The Transformation of the World Economy

New Directions and New Interests

THE UNITED NATIONS UNIVERSITY

STUDIES ON SOCIO-CULTURAL DEVELOPMENT ALTERNATIVES IN A CHANGING WORLD
General Editor: Anouar Abdel-Malek

The United Nations University's Project on Socio-cultural Development Alternatives in a Changing World (SCA), 1978-1982, arose from the deeply felt need to re-posit the problematique of human and social development in view of the dominant, Western-centred, reductionist models of development. The study concentrated on two major dimensions, constituting two sub-projects – Endogenous Intellectual Creativity and Transformation of the World – while select major thematic, innovative Convergence Areas (e.g., specificity and universality, geo-cultural visions of the world) were explored. Under the former theme development and its related issues were examined in terms of different geo-cultural areas of the world: Asia, Africa, the Arab World, Latin America, Europe, and North America. Under the latter sub-project consideration was given to the analysis of world transformation in the domains of science and technology, economy and society, culture and thought, religion and philosophy, and the making of a new international order.

The SCA series includes reports on collective research undertaken, its results and orientations, and theoretical studies on select themes, all aimed at the formulation of more realistic and sophisticated policies concerning the complex issue of development alternatives in a changing world.

TITLES IN THIS SERIES

THE UNITED NATIONS UNIVERSITY

STUDIES ON SOCIO-CULTURAL DEVELOPMENT
ALTERNATIVES IN A CHANGING WORLD

The Transformation of the World Economy

New Directions and New Interests

Tamás Szentes

The United Nations University
Tokyo

Zed Books Ltd
London and New Jersey

The Transformation of the World Economy was first published in 1988
by
Zed Books Ltd, 57 Caledonian Road, London N1 9BU, UK, and
171 First Avenue, Atlantic Highlands, New Jersey 07716, USA
and
The United Nations University, Toho Seimei Building,
15-1 Shibuya 2-chome, Shibuya-ku, Tokyo 150, Japan.

Cover designed by Lee Robinson.
Typeset by EMS Photosetters, Rochford, Essex.
Printed and bound in the United Kingdom
by Bookcraft Ltd., Bath, Avon

British Library Cataloguing in Publication Data

Szentes, Tamás, *1933–*
 The transformation of the world economy:
 new directions and new interests. — (The
 United Nations University Studies on socio-
 cultural development alternatives in
 a changing world; 3)
 1. Economic conditions
 I. Title   II. Series
 330.9'048

 ISBN 0-86232-726-1
 ISBN 0-86232-727-X Pbk

Library of Congress Cataloging-in-Publication Data

Szentes, Tamás.
 The transformation of the world economy: new
 directions and new interests/Tamás Szentes.
  p.   cm.
 Includes index.
 ISBN 0-86232-726-1. ISBN 0-86232-727-X (pbk.)
 1. Capitalism. 2. Economic history—1945–
 3. Developing countries—Economic conditions.
 I. Title.
 HB501.S99 1988
 330.9'048—dc19

Contents

1. Introduction

The transformation of the world towards a more democratic, just, peaceful and rational society is obviously a very complex and multi-dimensional process. It can by no means be equated with changes in the world economy only, nor can the latter be interpreted merely as shifts in the pattern of international commodity and financial flows.

The substance of the current transformation of the world we live in is a social transformation. This is naturally based upon changes in the economy but comprising the whole complex of social relations of production. These cannot be isolated from either technological changes (especially the new scientific and technological revolution) on the one hand, or from political, cultural and institutional changes on the other. It follows that the analysis of this world transformation requires a dialectical, holistic approach, which involves the complicated social science methodology of political economy rather than one based on the fragmentation of the social sciences. The latter, after all, were only the riposte of bourgeois ideology to the birth of Marxism in the 19th century, and produced 'pure economics' as the 'science' of economizing on costs, 'pure sociology' as the 'science' of behaviour patterns, 'pure political science' as the 'science' of political motivations, institutions, organizational patterns and forms, and 'pure historicism' as simple chronology.

A number of questions have to be raised when trying to understand this world transformation process, including very fundamental ones which inevitably invite different answers, depending on one's theoretical or ideological point of view. These questions include: What is actually changing? i.e. What system? And from what previous state to what new one? What is the scope and substance of the transformation process? Within what framework does it take place? How does the transformation proceed; what are its main motive forces? What is the role of economic changes in it? What kind of economy is it that is changing? At what stage of the transformation are we today, and what are the characteristics of this stage? What is the desired goal of the transformation process, and desired by whom? i.e. What kind of world system should be created? What is the present direction of changes, and does it promise to lead toward the desired goal? If not, what corrections or radical changes are needed, and who will carry them out? And so on.

These questions are related to the interpretation, explanation and value we place on particular social systems. In the present case, this means the historical development of capitalism, its essential nature and inherent laws of motion. This means understanding the national and international scene, the development and nature of the forces of the world economy, and also the characteristics of a post-capitalist society and how it might emerge.

As regards the desired goal of the transformation process, a certain consensus may appear despite ideological disagreements and conflicting interests. Most people may be able to agree on the general features of an ideal world society of the future. These might include equality among people; a high level of material and cultural welfare; peace and order; freedom, brotherhood and participatory democracy; ecological balance and environmental protection; the mastering of technologies, unfolding creativity and happiness etc. A consensus around these goals would not be surprising. For centuries humankind has been dreaming about a better future, better people, a better society, better living conditions and opportunities for all. A great many philosophers, scholars and theoreticians all over the world and throughout human history have, when trying to describe an imaginary better society of the future, drawn a somewhat similar picture. This is so whatever name they have given to it: whether they have called it heaven on earth, Paradise Regained, Utopia, Nova Atlantis, Socialism, Communism, or a post-materialist society. And the vision has been very similar regardless of whether they formulated their theses in religious or scientific terms.

The crucial difference and real conflict between the various views, theories and ideologies appears, however, once the question arises how the desired new society can be established. On·what economic and institutional basis? And by what social and political forces? For these are direct questions posed to existing, contemporary society. They imply a criticism of its nature as compared to that of the desired society. And they raise questions as to how far removed current reality is from the ideal, and what ways are open for its transformation.

Since the contemporary world consists of societies either inherited from or still dominated by capitalism — i.e. still bearing the marks of the capitalist system — the world transformation process cannot be properly understood without understanding the historical role, nature and development process of capitalism itself.

Contrary to the old, empirically defeated but still surviving apologia rooted in European classical economics, which conceives capitalism as the most rational and perfect form of society, and contrary, too, to those views which interpret it as an historical error, capitalism is neither the ideal summit of human evolution nor a dead end, but an organic part of the historical development of human society.

Its evolution — and its decline and downfall too — is not an historical accident, but an objective necessity deriving from the general tendencies of social development. Capitalism is a particular phase and not a blind alley or detour in the general development of human society. It represents a higher stage than any preceding social formation in the development of both the productive forces of society (i.e. labour force and its means of production) and the social relations of production (i.e. the social relations of ownership over the principal means of production and the distribution of social roles and incomes). No return to pre-capitalist social formations is historically feasible.

Capitalism has contributed to the progress of human society both by its great achievements and by the sharpening contradictions which it has produced but cannot solve:

⋆ It has developed science and technology, and the human productive forces in general — albeit not primarily for the benefit of the community as a whole, and certainly not under the control of the whole society;

⋆ It has developed nation states, national economies and societies, but only in certain parts of the world, while it has actually prevented, by oppression and exploitation, the rise and development of integrated national economies and societies in other parts;

⋆ It has developed an international economy and global division of labour, but in an asymmetrical pattern, with increasing inequalities between the participants; and it has set in motion an internationalization process parallel to the process of growing monopolization.

As with all social formations, capitalism constitutes an inter-related system of economic 'base', — i.e. the economic structure of society (which encompasses all the social relations of production in dialectical relationship with the productive forces) — and the corresponding 'superstructure' of political, legal and cultural institutions and ideas, including the various forms of social consciousness. In other words, a capitalist society implies the totality of economic, social, political and cultural phenomena and processes even if they always include some non-capitalist elements.

The most characteristic contradiction of this kind of society is the antagonism between labour and capital, i.e. between live, human labour, the creator of value and wealth on the one hand, and its dead, materialized, appropriated and capitalized product on the other. This contradiction manifests itself primarily in private ownership relations, and makes the rules for distributing social roles and income contradictory and dualistic. The principles that govern role allocation and income distribution for the working majority are not the same as those governing the minority of owners of capital.

The basic inequalities of the capitalist system become manifest both within the national framework and on the international scene: firstly, inequalities of ownership and control; secondly, inequalities in the allocation and distribution of roles within national societies as well as in the international division of labour; and thirdly, an unequal income distribution system which is basically the consequence of the above, both within national societies and within the world community.

Capitalism, whose emergence and operation presupposed from the outset a wider scope and sphere of activity than its immediate product, national economies, was the first system in history to bring about a world economy. The capitalist world economy involves relations of dominance and asymmetric dependence between its centre and its periphery.[1]

A natural concomitant of the operation of a world capitalist economy has been unequal development. One of its manifestations has been changes in the hierarchy among the developed capitalist countries of the centre and a shift of the leading role within it in favour of those countries which have succeeded at any given time in developing their productive forces and technology at a faster rate than others. Another — this time, cumulative — manifestation of unequal development has been the widening of the development gap between the centre and the periphery, i.e. the reproduction of relative underdevelopment. These two features are inter-related. The exploitation of the periphery provides the possibility (and at the same time a negative incentive — owing to protected markets limiting competition) to develop the productive forces in countries at the centre. In addition, the countries of the centre and the periphery are also connected by the marginal cases called 'semi-peripheries'[2] which are exposed simultaneously to the effect of both aspects. These marginal cases do not refute the dichotomy, the bipolarity, of the system, but are exactly indicative of its movement, development and change.

While capitalism has created and developed national economies in the central or core countries, it has prevented the countries of the periphery from developing their own national economies. Since the very birth of capitalism, therefore, a dialectical contradiction has appeared between national and international development, which capitalism has been unable to resolve.

Socio-economic development has been going ahead both at the level of nations, i.e. within countries, and on the world level. Consequently, it is not sufficient to have a single unit of analysis. It does in certain circumstances make sense to analyse development processes within a national framework, i.e. on a country level, because not all the socio-economic processes of individual countries are related directly to the global system. The existence and relevance of national economies and societies have not disappeared yet, and in fact cannot fade away as long as the national character of the political superstructure of the state and its institutions survives.

On the other hand, internationalization is forging ahead and strengthens the global content of the development process. A world-level analysis[3] helps to understand many new, specific problems. It is also, of course, a pre-requisite for understanding the unequal development of the world capitalist system, centre–periphery relations, and the causes of the underdevelopment of the Third World.[4]

Since capitalism has developed both within national boundaries as a national system, and as an international or world system, the appropriate unit of its analysis is neither exclusively the national nor the world system. The acceptance of these two equally relevant and real units of analysis clearly points to the need for action, too, on both these levels, i.e. the dialectical relationship between national and international politics. It is equally wrong to seek for solutions only at the national level and forget about what changes are required in the world economy as a whole, as it is to focus only on the international level and leave the required national changes out of account.

The capitalist system involves both its fundamental social contradiction (the antagonism between labour and capital) which makes a social class struggle of varying intensity inevitable, and the contradiction between national development and the process of internationalization (based upon dominance and monopolization) which gives birth to national movements of oppressed, exploited peoples. It follows that the social (class) and national movements make up the primary forces of transformation. These interact and mingle with each other, either reinforcing or weakening their impact. State power is the main instrument they both seek to control. Since the role and interests of the different social or class forces in national movements also vary, the class content of the nation state becomes a decisive factor not only from the point of view of social progress but also of national development.

A post-capitalist society, whatever name is used to define it, has to resolve all the contradictions inherent in capitalism. It has not only to develop science and technology further but also to put them under the control of the community as a whole and make them serve the purposes of social welfare and satisfy the real needs of working people. It has to end the antagonistic contradiction between labour and capital by changing the social relations of production and socializing ownership and control over the means of production. It has to promote and carry out a real internationalization by eliminating, first, the dominance of certain nations over others and, second, ensuring equal opportunities for the development and full sovereignty of all nations.

The fulfilment of tasks like these requires, of course, a long historical period which can be described as a process of liberation or emancipation. This multi-faceted process involves the liberation of human beings from the domination of nature and the dominance of what they themselves have produced — technology, wealth, and power. It requires the liberation of society from group and class dominance, exploitation and alienation (i.e. social emancipation); the liberation of nations from the dominance of others (i.e. national emancipation); and finally, the liberation of the whole world from the dangers of war, self-destruction and ecological deterioration.

The liberation of human beings and their societies from the dominance of nature requires an appropriate development and social management of science and technology. Their liberation from their own alienated products and of society from class dominance and exploitation requires fundamental changes in ownership, control and power relations within the societies concerned. The liberation of nations requires not only formal political independence but also economic sovereignty and cultural identity. And the liberation of the world from the dangers of destruction requires not only a military balance of power and specific anti-pollution measures, but the elimination of the fundamental causes of violent international conflicts — the military–industrial complex as well as the basic inequalities in international relations — and a global ecological policy.

Post-capitalist society, namely socialism, is supposed in turn to be a transitional stage towards a really worldwide and communal (communist) society. But precisely because capitalism has been unable to complete the internationalization process and produce a really transnational world system, while, on the other hand, it has actually prevented the rise of national economies in certain parts of the world, the emerging socialist systems confront a particularly onerous task. They have to face not only the job of eliminating class inequalities and the great many social, cultural and moral distortions inherited from capitalism (while preserving and transcending its very real historical achievements), but also the double task of developing a national economy (or even creating it where it has not yet been able to arise) and at the same time completing the process of internationalization.

Owing to the uneven development of capitalism in different parts of the world and the multi-dimensional, complex character of social development, the process of transforming the system is necessarily also uneven. The transition to socialism in certain spheres may begin along with the further development of capitalism in others. Socialist systems may arise, as they did historically, in some parts of the world while capitalism survives in or continues to penetrate other regions. All this makes for an increasingly mixed world in which differing economic elements conflict with and also influence one another.

Since capitalism has in this century lost its worldwide hegemony, it cannot operate in the same way as before due to the existence of new, socialist systems. Nor can the latter develop in the same manner as they could have if they had not been surrounded by capitalist countries, threatening them militarily, and if they had not had to work in a basically capitalist world economy. The very fact that socialist development has historically started as a *partial* world process — i.e. in single countries, and not as a universal, worldwide process — has had many implications. So has the fact that socialism started in relatively less developed, peripheral or semi-peripheral countries, overshadowed by the presence of economically much more advanced capitalist countries which exerted an impact and various demonstration effects (both positive and negative). These conditions created certain specific difficulties and contradictions, as well as facilitating factors, for the development of socialism.

At the same time, the rise of new socialist systems spread over a considerable part of the world and the birth of new, independent nation states in all the peripheral areas of world capitalism have increasingly influenced the socio-economic processes in the advanced capitalist countries, themselves. Between the different parts of our global society there has been also increasing co-operation at various levels — the United Nations, the multilateral and regional organizations, and bilateral collaboration in the economic, technological, scientific, cultural and educational fields. If these are based on mutual interest or compromises made necessary by the urgent global problems that need to be solved, these forms of co-operation can actually ensure a peaceful coexistence and even push forward the global process of emancipation beyond the changes taking place in, or originating from, individual parts of the world.

The world transformation process, therefore, involves both local changes — i.e. transformations going ahead in parallel in individual parts of the world, these being in both mutually beneficial and contradictory interaction with each other — and changes in the whole — i.e. the transformation of the global society of humankind, making for advances at the world level.

2. Changing Theories of the World Economy

Leaving aside the minimum consensus which can be found concerning the most general features of an ideal society for the future, the theoretical approaches to understanding society differ widely. These affect how one assesses the currently prevailing society, the system to be transformed, and the definition of the ways, concrete direction and leading forces of such a transformation. Differences in theoretical approach will also affect judgements as to the nature, rules, basis and structure of the social system which may grow out of the transformation.

The development of the capitalist system has been accompanied by the rise of various pro- or anti-capitalistic theories connected with particular social forces and political movements. There was the romantic anti-capitalism which opposed the penetration of capitalist relations in pre-capitalist societies and that wanted to defend or even restore these societies. In addition, numerous socialist ideas came into being — utopian, reformist and revolutionary alike — challenging the ideological protagonists of capitalism. As a consequence, however, of the expansion of capitalism and its harsh realities, most of the romantic anti-capitalist ideas as well as utopian socialist theories have disappeared (only to re-emerge temporarily later or elsewhere whenever a choice of development alternatives is on the agenda). But the changes in the internal structure and external dimensions of the capitalist system have always induced its main opponents — the labour movement — and the main anti-capitalistic ideology — Marxism — to renew the argument. It must be said, however, that such critiques must take into account actual changes; dogmatic orthodoxy which rigidly insists on old-fashioned theses related to another time or place cannot survive for long.

This book cannot present, of course, an overall survey of the great many ideologies in contention, or even just the main schools of economic thought,[5] partly because its size is limited as is the knowledge of its author, and partly because it intends to deal with the actual process of transformation, and especially with the recent changes in the world economy. Having said that, it seems necessary to include here at least some comparative investigation of the different and changing theories of the world economy. Though it is difficult to draw a sharp division between the different theories, we have to categorize the great many diverse views — even at the expense of considerable simplification — in order to point to the main differences in respect of certain key issues which are relevant to the transformation process.

We ought to note that, owing to the increasingly mixed character of the world economy (i.e. the heterogeneous nature and varying position of the different countries participating in world economic processes), the theories concerned vary and cross-cut one another much more than those theories of social systems which can be distinguished as either pro- or anti-capitalist conceptions.

We should also note that since capitalism as a national system first arose in Western Europe and as an international system radiated out from there, the first and still dominant theories of both how capitalist national economies work and international economic relations reflect West European conditions and Western capitalist interests. These theories dominated and mostly replaced other pre-capitalist economic ideas and made the development of economic theories later or in other countries more or less derivative. However, capitalism has never been realized as a 'pure', totally homogeneous system either at national level (with society consisting only of two classes — capitalist owners and workers owning only their labour power which they sell) or at the world level (as a perfectly dichotomous system embracing only an exploiting advanced centre and an exploited underdeveloped periphery). The survival of various other elements, intermediate or marginal strata, provides a permanent breeding ground for the existence of other ideologies. Many of them are rooted in pre-capitalist or non-European cultures. They represent not only a valuable cultural heritage from the past and a great enrichment of the culture of humanity in general, but also important additional forces in the system. None of them, of course, has remained completely insulated from capitalist reality or fully independent of the dominant capitalist ideology, or its main antagonist.

It is true that certain antecedent ideas of classical Western economics can be found in non-West European history. Moreover, numerous basic principles and methods were first discovered elsewhere — for example, the concept of labour-determined value in ancient Arab and also Greek culture. Nevertheless the dominant capitalist system has made its own body of theory dominant and forced all others to relate to it, either as followers or opponents. Even Marxism, which arose as the ideology of the victims of West European capitalism — both local proletariats and exploited working people overseas, made use of British classical economics as a source, and articulated its anti-theses in response to the latter when formulating its universal anti-capitalist theory and outlining the historic processes which would lead to a post-capitalist world society.

As capitalism has developed and its international patterns changed, the foci and issues of dominant capitalist theory, as well as of its counter-theories, have shifted to reflect both new stages of capitalist development in general and the actual position of particular countries in the context of the world economy.

Such modifications, however, do not result in a perfectly adequate theory. Equally, the theory may not be relevant to particular local conditions only, since by reflecting the position of the parts of the world economy, it may indirectly reflect the development of the world economy as a whole. This explains why so many attempts to produce a genuine, totally independent theory valid only for a given country, continent or culture have always failed in the same way as the attempts which neglect the specific conditions in a given country or a given period end up trying to put a uniform straitjacket on the unique conditions of particular countries.

Since the universal appears in particularities and the particular makes up the universal, the development of theories reflects, in a contradictory way, the development both of the particular parts and of the universal whole of a system.

Besides, theories have developed also according to their own internal logic, as well as in confrontation with each other and harsh reality, not to forget the personal qualities of their authors. Objectively, the social content and orientation of a given theory may be quite different or even diametrically opposed to the subjective feelings, wishes and personal class position, nationality or group interest of its author. We all know that an objectively pro-capitalist, bourgeois conception does not necessarily mean that its author is also a capitalist or a conscious protagonist of capitalism.

All these circumstances make a critical survey of economic theories difficult. But in the very process of trying, it becomes obvious that theories of the world economy will differ fundamentally according to whether they are based upon pro- or anti-capitalist ideologies and, secondly, on whether they are elaborated from the viewpoint of the advanced centre of the world economy or its underdeveloped periphery.

Finally, we should also note here that periphery-motivated views are not necessarily anti-capitalist, nor are the theories produced in the centre of world capitalism necessarily pro-capitalist. In general, ideological frontiers never coincide with geographical ones.

The History of Conventional Theories[6]

Mercantilism
Apart from some early theoretical forerunners, in Europe and outside, on economic relations between individual countries or the various parts of empires, the first sophisticated theory on international economic relations as well as the economic growth of nations was mercantilism. Mercantilism was the product, primarily though not exclusively, of the historical transformation which led from a feudalism that was collapsing to industrial capitalism. It reflected, and also directly served by formulating a mercantilist economic policy, the interests of the so-called primitive accumulation of capital and national industrialization. Primitive capital accumulation was both the process by which producers were deprived of their means of production, and also the process of the accumulation of capital in money form, the artificial process of 'manufacturing the manufactures', and last but not least, a process of robbing and commercially exploiting other countries and the worldwide expansion of merchant capital.

Attributing the growth of national wealth to the accumulation of 'real money' (precious metals), mercantilism in its early Spanish and Portuguese variant undoubtedly came under the influence of the fetish of money. This was the illusion of exchange value as against real use value, and the illusion of money as against ordinary commodities.

This illusion, however, perfectly reflected not only the actual reality of the primitive accumulation process but also the fetishism characteristic of the entire history of capitalism, of the commodity and money worlds, which makes most human relations appear to be relations between things, and which conceals class relations by exchange relations.

Mercantilist theory proposed an aggressive foreign trade policy to acquire surplus, in money form, through unequal exchanges with other nations. At home the consequent inflow of precious metals gave a boost, via a price explosion, to the expansion of the domestic market and commodity production. Potential capital began to be concentrated and a start was thereby given to a capitalist national economy. At the same time, the positive balance of trade that mercantilist policy intended to ensure by the export of the new protected manufactures, contributed a lot to the rise of British dominance in the international economy that was in the making.

Mercantilism frankly represented the idea of unequal exchange from which the dominant nation benefited, and so the concept of the inequality of partners in the growing capitalist international economy. It also frankly advocated state intervention in the economic process and the use of institutional measures, including subsidies and protectionism.

While mercantilism as a theory has been ousted from the conventional world of pro-capitalist economics, to be replaced by the euphemistic, even rather apologetic ideas of free trade, liberalism and *laissez-faire* that first appeared with the Physiocrats but which were expressed later in a sophisticated way by classical economics, it has survived in practice in the economic policies of late-comers which have sought to protect and promote their infant industries. Moreover a mercantilist thread of policy can even be detected in the practice of the principal advocates of liberalism.

Physiocratism

Physiocratism, born in France, was a reflection of the failure of mercantilist policy in that country which was lagging behind Britain in international competition. It was also the theoretical expression of the beginning of the capitalist transformation process in agriculture. As the representatives of a relatively less successful nation in international trade, the French physiocrats appeared as the advocates of equality in international trade and of a rather inward-looking national economic policy. Besides rejecting state intervention, particularly the subsidized expansion of industrial exports, and calling for liberalism in general, they pointed to some of the possible dangers and disadvantages of international trade.

Without questioning the potential advantages of an international division of labour, they put emphasis on domestic equilibrium, in particular on the development of agriculture which would physically increase the available volume of consumer goods, and on the subordination of export policy to the import needs arising from the insufficiency of domestic production as a result of natural conditions.

Mercantilism and physiocratism, as we can see, appear as the early variants of certain well-known pairs of opposed, but equally biased, one-sided concepts of development policy: outward- versus inward-orientation; export-oriented industrialization versus import-substitution; growth-oriented versus equilibrium-ensuring economic policy; industrialization versus agricultural development, etc. And also of the two opposed principles (both of which miss the crucial issue) of international trade: inequality versus equality in exchange relations.

The two bodies of theory also represent, in an opposite way, the lack of understanding at the time of the double nature of the two, inter-related aspects of commodity production, as well as the ignorance of the dialectical unity and contradiction of the national and international realization of capitalism. It is this lack of understanding which has become characteristic of non-Marxian economics throughout its history.

While mercantilism overemphasized one side of the dialectical unity — the process of exchange versus production, exchange value versus use value, accumulated money versus the consumable commodities, and international sources versus national ones for capitalist development — physiocratism overrated the other side. But both schools formulated their theoretical principles, the rules of the economic game, as equally valid for the national and the international economy.

Classical Economics

Contrary to these two schools, classical economics made a certain, but extremely important exception, in the case of the international economy, to its own principles elaborated for the national economy. While the labour theory of value principle (i.e. the determination of relative prices of goods in accordance with the relative labour inputs involved in the production of the commodities concerned) was the central element of the classical or Ricardian theory of the national economy, the same principle was not regarded as applicable to its concept of international trade. No doubt, the labour theory of value, even in its early pre-Marxian formulation, necessarily revealed a conflict of class interests, at least in the distribution of the total product of labour. By eliminating it from international trade theory, classical economics could easily present its thesis of the harmony of interests in the international economy and of the equal benefits that ostensibly flowed from the international division of labour if *laissez-faire* were ensured.

Though it was actually the interests of the first, strongest, and most advanced nation of industrial capitalism that the classical British economists expressed in their theses on international economics, they made an appearance of representing the common interests of all countries, including the weaker partners in international trade.

The most elaborate and consistent version (as compared to that of Adam Smith or John Stuart Mill) of classical economics, namely the Ricardian theory, drew a naïvely optimistic and increasingly unrealistic picture of the capitalist world economy.

Ricardo, just like Smith, assumed that, if capitalist entrepreneurs in national economies as well as capitalist nations in their international economic relations, could follow and realize their own selfish interests free from any institutional intervention or obstacles, then the final outcome would be the best for everybody, the maximum possible welfare, and the optimum for resource allocation. The 'invisible hand' of the market would have triumphed.

His theory on the international economy was based upon the idea of a system in perfect equilibrium kept in operation by perfectly correlated, spontaneous flows of commodities and money between the partner national economies which would also be in perfect equilibrium, and upon the idea (undoubtedly brilliant *per se*) of comparative advantages and costs.

Ricardo's views incorporated the numerous naïve assumptions involved in the classical concept of national equilibrium. These included Adam Smith's dogma about the division of the total value of production into incomes; the necessary harmony between production and consumption; the quantity theory of money; the automatic equilibrium mechanism of saving and investment, of capital supply and demand; and the equilibrium mechanism of labour supply and demand as a result of subsistence minimum wages and demographic changes. But the Ricardian equilibrium view of the international economy was made even more unrealistic by its neglect of those cases where the participating national economies were in disequilibrium or in 'imperfect equilibrium'. The theory also excluded the case of more or less permanent debtor–creditor relations, the flows of money as capital, and the inequalities in power relations that exist — i.e. international dominance and dependence.

The classical theory of comparative advantage, which was used to support the ideological struggle waged by an increasingly powerful English bourgeoisie for the repeal of the Corn Laws which served the interests of the landlords, suggested an international division of labour which would develop in accordance with national comparative costs. The basis of this was an international comparison of the relative labour costs in different countries of two or more products, their relative costs being measured in terms of one another. Alternatively, a national comparison of the relative international price of two or more commodities would be made, their relative price being expressed in that of another country. Accordingly, if each of the partner countries specialized in the production of that particular commodity which ensured the greatest absolute advantage, or the smallest absolute disadvantage, then, as a result of such international division of labour, both the economies of individual partner countries and the world economy would benefit. The former would have available quantities of the products exceeding their own productive capacities, and total world output and world income would increase substantially.

Ricardo, without taking properly into account technological progress, assumed that the production function was basically or exclusively determined by natural conditions. This would make production functions, i.e. the output increments resulting from additional units of labour input, vary from product to product and from country to country. He made other mistakes too, such as neglecting the relevance of infrastructural development, the possibility of external and internal economies of scale, the differences between skilled and unskilled labour, and direct and indirect linkages and spread effects. In short, he disregarded the dynamics of the social productive forces in their broad sense. He overlooked also the possible natural, institutional and technological monopolies that could arise in the production of certain commodities. He ignored the impact of variations in size and structurally different development potentials of individual national economies. All these elements made the theory of comparative advantage extremely vulnerable, static and over-simplified — failings which were compounded by some of his other assumptions which, however justified originally, later became anachronistic, as for example was the case with his premise of the international immobility of capital.

This latter factor needs highlighting. Under the conditions of international flows of investment capital, the debtor–creditor relationship has increasingly ceased to be merely a temporary consequence or an attendant phenomenon of sales contracts. It has become a determinant of the latter, which finds expression, together with other factors, in the phenomenon of cumulative indebtedness. The international mobility of capital has also undermined the Ricardian picture of the world economy in another respect. The idea of all national economies specializing according to their comparative advantage implicitly assumes that the calculations of comparative cost are made on the macro or national level and that the decisions on the allocation of productive resources are also taken at that level. But the 'invisible hand' does not guarantee a perfect correspondence between micro and macro level processes. Also, in any case, these calculations and decisions are made by independent, sovereign national entities developing in compliance with their internal needs.

These implicit assumptions came into sharp contradiction with the reality of the development of the world capitalist system in which a great many countries had been deprived of independence by colonialism. In reality, the international division of labour by no means developed in accordance with comparative costs computed for national economies, not even in the case of the independent or dominant countries. In general, international specialization within the capitalist world economy has developed according to the business interests and profit calculations of private capital. Moreover, in the case of the dependent peripheral countries, it has been shaped in accordance with the interests of *foreign* powers and primarily foreign capital, which results from the export of private capital from the more developed, dominant capitalist countries.

Despite its obvious shortcomings, naïve assumptions and increasingly anachronistic premises, the classical theory of international economics has survived through a long history of modifications and corrections. Even today, it remains the pillar of conventional, conservative views of the international economic order. While the labour theory of value of classical theory has become evil-sounding (since Marxism made use of it to prove exploitation and class conflict), and has disappeared for ever from pro-capitalist, conventional theories of how national economies work, the classical theory of international trade and product specialization, with its full trust in spontaneous market forces and capitalist entrepreneurship, has proved to be perfectly suitable to serve — at least as a set of slogans — the interests of private capital of the strongest nations. What this theory suggested as a recipe to lead to a better world was supposed to be a transformation process in which each country would develop its own competitive national capitalism and eliminate all restrictions on market forces, while adjusting its production structure in practice to that of the most developed nation.

The various corrections and modifications made to the classical theory of international economics by neo-classical and other schools of thought taking into account technological progress and international capital mobility, may have reformulated some of its postulates, but have hardly made the picture of a harmonious world economy more realistic.

Without dwelling on the details, let us look at a few of the perhaps most characteristic and important cases of the reformulation of the original classical dogmas, marking the further evolution of conventional theory.

Alfred Marshall

Marshall elaborated a special theory[7] for the international economy which has actually made the separation of the principles valid for national economies from those governing international economic relations even sharper and more explicit than Ricardo. Besides neglecting — among other things — the effects of external economic relations on internal ones (productivity, the price and demand relationship, and so on), Marshall reduced the question of international equilibrium to the rather doubtful concept of the point of intersection of reciprocal demand curves. These curves were drawn on the basis of assuming certain given, but not objectively determined price relations and demand elasticities. This concept paved the way for a mathematically accurate formulation of equilibrium conditions, of great interest to academics and their mathematical manipulations, but bearing little relationship to the real world.

The neo-classical picture of the capitalist world economy has retained the concept of a general equilibrium automatically restoring itself, and also the assumed equality and independence of the partners. Though the reformulated equilibrium concept took into account technological progress and economies of scale, the presumed harmony of interests was supposed to be unaffected or rather reinforced by these conditions.

On the basis of marginal productivity theory, the principle of comparative advantage and the concept of a rational system for the international allocation of resources have been modified without, however, any radical change in the final naïve conclusions. The revised conception reflected the relatively decreased significance, in the industralized countries, of the natural endowments which Ricardo had considered to be the determinants of national production functions. Emphasis was now placed on the relative scarcity or abundance of labour and capital in individual countries, which determined a rational system of division of labour accordingly. Each country, it was now argued, if following its best self-interest and allowing spontaneous market forces to operate, would specialize in those branches of production which would ensure the greatest absorption of whichever factor of production, capital or labour, was most abundant (therefore relatively low priced). In other words and expressed in the terms of conventional economics, the capital-rich countries ought to specialize in capital-intensive industries, while the capital-short countries, which have a labour surplus, ought to specialize in labour-intensive activities. Their comparative advantages now lay in the respective abundant factor.

Such a rational system of international specialization was supposed to arise not only as a result of the domestic mechanism for the spontaneous orientation of factors of production within individual national economies, but also owing to international factor mobility, particularly international flows of investment capital. This postulate is expressed in the famous thesis of B. Ohlin and E. F. Heckscher.[8]

The classical concept of international economic equilibrium has been completed by the premise of international factor mobility. The revised concept assumes that capital tends to flow from the countries which are rich in capital (where the marginal productivity of capital is low and capital is undervalued) to the countries suffering capital shortage. As a result, the international distribution of capital resources gets equalized and so do national productivity and income levels. Accordingly, the capitalist world economy, if based upon the free activity of private capital both inside and outside its national economies, and on the free flow of money, commodities and factors of production, would operate not only as an automatic equilibrium system but would also bring about an equalization among its parts, a process which would automatically eliminate the underdevelopment of certain countries. The best policy, therefore, to promote the transformation of the world into this desired state is the 'open door policy', i.e. the elimination of all institutional obstacles to the inflow of foreign capital and the guaranteeing of its safe, uncontrolled and unrestricted activity.

All these assumptions and policies correspond perfectly with conventional economics' interpretation of the underdevelopment of Third World countries. This is conceived as a simple lagging behind, a quantitatively measurable difference in development level (such as *per capita* GDP), and as a natural but lower stage of the normal and general process of economic growth.[9] Conventional explanations trace this back merely to unfavourable local conditions, internal limiting factors of growth.[10]

If underdevelopment is only a relative backwardness stemming from internal factors, which the capitalist forces of the international economy can help to overcome, then, of course, the developing countries, without blaming external factors, should trust in the spontaneous operation of the capitalist world economy.

The idyllic picture of the capitalist world economy, drawn first by classical economics and completed later — as we have seen — by the neo-classical and marginalist schools, has not been fundamentally revised even by the Keynesian Revolution of conventional economics, even though the latter has theoretically undermined the classical premise of the perfect equilibrium of national economies without state intervention. More recently, neo-liberalism has attacked even the Keynesian revision of the classical dogmas, and gained influence again in the most developed capitalist countries (particularly in the USA), despite the successful application of the Keynesian recipe in post-war economic policy. Little wonder that the conventional theory of international economics has remained the dominant theory for the centre of world capitalism.

Apart from Marxism, which since its very birth has been rejecting all the fundamental postulates and theses of conventional pro-capitalist economics, it is only the new school of a few progressive economists belonging to or sympathizing with the poor nations of the Third World, and called, whether correctly or not, the advocates of *dependency theory*,[11] which has broken with the conventional dogmas of international economics.

Though Marxism has also produced a dependency theory on under-development, and its conclusions often coincide with the conclusions of the new school,[12] particularly in their critique of the conventional view and how to characterize prevailing conditions in the world economy, a distinction can perhaps be made on the basis that the new dependency school is anti-imperialist but not generally anti-capitalist and it suggests a different way of transforming the world compared to the way proposed by Marxism. Some of the leading theoreticians of the new school, the reformists, criticize only imperialist practice, dominance and monopolies, without criticizing the capitalist system as such although it is the root cause. They also tend to call for substantial reforms in international economic relations without demanding a full transformation of the national system of economy and society, too. Others, the New Left or radicals, advocate a global transformation by way of a world revolution or an international struggle by the poor 'South' against the rich 'North'.

Reformist and New Left Theories[13]

Development Economics and the *Dependencia* School

A new school of economic thought arose after the Second World War, in the period when, along with substantial changes in international political relations, the deep economic and social problems of the developing countries (both those inherited from colonialism and those emerging under the changed conditions) came to the fore.

It is no accident that the most outstanding representatives of the new school, whether belonging to a developing or a developed nation — such as Raul Prebisch and Celso Furtado, or Gunnar Myrdal and Hans Singer respectively — were all involved in a job, often with the UN, or a research activity, related to the underdeveloped regions when they began to rethink and critically reinvestigate the conventional economic doctrines. Nothing else has contra-dicted these doctrines more effectively than the history and empirical reality of the underdeveloped parts of the world economy.

The major work in this critical revision was done in the late fifties and early sixties. This was a time when the most acute problem seemed to be the decreasing share and weakening bargaining position in international trade of the developing countries. Their terms of trade were deteriorating, indebtedness was beginning to spiral, and they were becoming very obviously reliant in financial and technological terms on the advanced countries. The result was that, at first, this new school placed a somewhat exaggerated importance on certain surface phenomena and processes in the capitalist world economy.

Rejecting conventional dogmas about the automatically self-righting equilibrium system and equalizing mechanisms of the international economy, the representatives of the new school (led by Myrdal[14]) pointed to certain irreversible processes and to the equilibrium-disturbing and cumulatively disequalizing effects of spontaneous market forces in general. What they did not reveal, however, was the real nature of these market forces rooted in the capitalist system. As a result and despite the great merit of the new lines of argument, a certain illusion was created, namely that it would be possible to regulate these market forces effectively and this would solve the problem and perfect the system without radically transforming it.

The first important achievement of the new school was its denial that the actual development of the international division of labour had in practice been in line with the principle of comparative advantage or that in the real world of international economic relations equal and sovereign partners were co-operating with each other and gaining equal benefits and advantages from international trade and specialization. The new school of thought drew attention to the disadvantages of the type of specialization which had been imposed on the developing countries (see, for example, the Singer thesis[15]). They pointed out the regular losses suffered by the latter in international trade (Prebisch and Lewis[16]). They revealed the relations of domination that existed in the world economy and the corresponding dependence of the developing countries — for example, Balogh's thesis on unequal partners,[17] Prebisch's on trade dependence,[18] Furtado's and Singer's on cultural and technological ties,[19] and Perroux on structural dependence.[20]

However, the explanations placed, in most cases, too great an emphasis and responsibility on one or another *partial* factor, or some temporary and ambiguous condition. To take one example, the unfavourable patterns of specialization forced on the Third World were originally, and for the given historical period understandably, identified with particular types of product, i.e. their use value. The argument was very much restricted to the case of primary products. This meant that the new theory could neither make the case for improving the world market position of certain primary producers, nor argue the negative consequences of a certain type of limited or distorted industralization. As a consequence, the new theory also needed to be revised which, however, led to a complete denial of the importance of the choice of product type and production branch in specialization (as in the thesis of Singer II[21]).

The deterioration of the terms of trade, particularly as measured by the simplest, barter formula, was stressed so much as the main problem of the Third World in general that international inequality and exploitation were often interpreted as merely an inequality of exchange relations. This meant denying that the improvement of terms of trade in some other periods could substantially alter the basically unfavourable position of the developing countries; whilst at the same time overlooking the fact that deteriorated terms of trade had not prevented some advanced industrial countries in the past from carrying out a vigorous economic growth and improving their position in the world economy.

When explaining the deterioration of the terms of trade and shedding light on the disguised regular drain of income from the developing countries as a result of international trade (namely the transfer from them of the benefits of productivity increases and technological progress), the new school often referred to such factors as the demonstration effect, technological disparities and currency devaluations resulting in lower export prices and lower relative wage levels, as causes of the demand elasticity of exported commodities. A low price elasticity of demand, however, can be both advantageous and disadvantageous, depending on the direction of price changes. It has turned out to be a condition not only for a decrease in export revenues, as in the case of many primary products experiencing a falling price, but also for a successful pricing policy and increase in income (at least temporarily) of producer associations like OPEC. In addition, some primary commodities are also exported by developed countries, whose share in the world market for primary products actually increased in the fifties and sixties.

Similarly, the explanation for unequal exchange and deviations in the international distribution of income from what might be expected from productivity ratios, in terms of the differences in the bargaining power of countries or of their working classes, was built on very weak foundations. Without answering the question — what determines the difference in the bargaining power of partner countries, and the discrepancy between income and productivity ratios (which, of course, requires a much deeper analysis of the entire socio-economic structure) — such an explanation leads either to the dubious tautological formula that weaker countries always lose out against stronger ones, whatever product they exchange, just because they are weaker,[22] or to the strange, New Left theory of imperialism[23] which traces back the underdevelopment and exploitation of the developing nations to the successful wage struggle of the working class in the developed countries.

The complexities of the economic dependence of the periphery and the dominant position of the centre are mostly interpreted by the new school as a dependence manifested primarily in trade relations or in the transfer of technologies and consumption patterns etc. The most direct form of economic dependence and dominance, namely the foreign ownership and control of the commanding heights of the economy, is usually more or less neglected, despite the role of foreign monopoly capital in shaping production and trade structures, technological and consumption patterns etc.

The new school has refrained from presenting an overall critique of the activity of foreign monopoly capital and its origins, motivations and general role in the contemporary world capitalist system. Instead, it has merely rejected the theses of conventional economic theory on the international mobility of capital, both in respect of the alleged 'natural' direction of capital flows and its idealized positive effects; it has pointed instead to the 'perverse' movement of capital (Balogh, 1963) and some of the undesired, harmful consequences of foreign investments.[24] The new school has also emphasized certain partial, though important, phenomena or temporary effects such as the dangers of political interference and the disadvantages, for local entrepreneurs, which follow from 'too early' an inflow of foreign investments,[25] or from the 'package' character of foreign direct investment. But all these limited critiques and lines of analysis have allowed some illusions still to remain, including that foreign investors are amenable to correcting their behaviour and even that a harmony between their interests and those of domestic capitalists is possible.

The theoreticians of the new school have also called in doubt the conventional assumptions about the equal opportunities for technological progress flowing from specialization, and about the levelling effects of the international transfer of technology. They have pointed to the unequal effects on technological development arising from the different types of specialization (Singer, 1964) and to the losses incurred by technologically underdeveloped countries, which follow from the repeated adjustments involved in adapting foreign technology (Balogh, 1963), or from the inappropriate character of the technology transferred from the advanced countries (Singer, 1971).

What, however, seems to diminish the great value of these results, is again that the problem of technology is often taken out of the overall socio-economic context, or even that the nature of technology is treated as a primary factor. This is the case when the structural dualism, heterogeneity or disintegration of the underdeveloped countries' economies are attributed to a technological dualism, and not vice versa (Furtado, 1971), or when the ultimate source of all the troubles of the underdeveloped countries, particularly their increasing unemployment, is seen as the inappropriate technology imported from the advanced countries reflecting the latters' factor endowments rather than local conditions (Singer, 1971). Such views — however important and real the problems they touch on — easily lead to the completely erroneous practice of assessing employment effects on the micro level — i.e. calculating the number of jobs created by a given technology and leaving out of consideration the indirect effects via input and output linkages on the macro level. Another consequence is to give a spurious validity to the idea that has appeared in some New Left or pseudo-Marxist writings according to which the technology transferred manifests a definite class content which can determine the nature of social relations in the underdeveloped country concerned.

These and the similar cases mentioned before clearly show certain weaknesses in the reformist variant of the *Dependencia* School and also its close theoretical, though not necessarily political, relationship with radical New Left versions. As regards the latter, perhaps the most outstanding theory exemplifying all the controversies, ambiguities and errors which follow from trying to analyse the international system through its exchange relations instead of its production relations is Emmanuel's theory of unequal exchange.

Arghiri Emmanuel and the New Left

Emmanuel, substituting a theory of trade imperialism for Lenin's theory of investment imperialism, identifies modern imperialism with the dominance of certain countries embodied in their strong bargaining position in the world market and the exploitation carried out as a result of trade relations between unequal partners in the world economy. He considers unequal exchange as the characteristic form of exploitation and, in the final analysis, international disparities in wages as the cause of this inequality in international trade, and hence ultimately of the unequal development of the different parts of world capitalism.

International differences in wage rates are an undoubted fact. The consequently heightened marketing problems are reflected in the relatively new phenomenon of 'run-away industries', the tendency of multinational corporations to establish subsidiaries abroad, the competition of low wage-cost commodities in the world market as well as the pressure for protectionist measures from certain Western trade union and even business groups. These facts have persuaded other Marxist authors — among them Oscar Braun, Jagdish Saigal and Samir Amin[26] — to assign a specific role to, or at least place emphasis on, wage differences in the analysis of international economic relations. But it is only Emmanuel who has gone to the lengths of building a whole theory of world market price formation on international wage rates as an independent variable. In order to do that, he has needed, of course, to regard all the other factors, including the consequences of the ownership and controlling positions of foreign monopoly capital and the international investments of multinational corporations, as of secondary importance. He has also had to work out a new general prices and wages theory applicable to national economies. (Ironically he made use of Marx's political economy for this purpose!)

The basic postulate underlying Emmanuel's theory is that the international mobility of capital ensures an equalization of national profit rates, while the relative immobility of labour prevents a parallel equalization of wage rates. He holds, contrary to the Marxian theory of prices, that production prices which result, in general, from capital mobility and profit rate equalization, are determined by wages as independent variables. Thus he concludes that the difference in bargaining power of different countries' workers causes wage levels in the centre and the periphery to diverge, and so makes their relative export prices uneven.

Emmanuel's postulate actually suggests that unequal exchange (i.e. exploitation and imperialism) would not exist if the international mobility of capital was paralleled by an equivalent mobility of labour. This assumption fits perfectly with the old dogmas of conventional economics about perfect equilibrium and harmony resulting from perfect factor mobility.

This narrow approach reduces the varied forms of inequality of exchange relations, as well as international inequality and exploitation in general, to a single case, namely the inequality of wage rates accompanied by equalized profit rates, and explains it by reference to a single factor: 'the monopoly position of the working classes of the developed countries'.

This assumed equalization of profit rates between centre and periphery also assumes an equality in power between the capital of the periphery and that of the centre, and neglects completely any difference in nature between capital flowing from the centre to the periphery and the capital or income flowing in the opposite direction. In other words, Emmanuel neglects the very fact of the underdevelopment of the periphery as far as its capital is concerned. By excluding the role of capital in the formation of the international 'price scissor' and in the exploitation of the periphery, he regards the very factor which has shaped the asymmetric structure of the capitalist world economy to be neutral. He attaches no importance to the international manifestations of the fundamental form of capitalist exploitation, i.e. profit-making. He does not see its role in the local accumulation of profits and their repatriation as a result of the foreign investments of monopoly capital. He disregards the losses flowing from one-sided specialization, monopoly prices dictated by international corporations, the formation of different prices as a result of the uneven development of the productive forces and the composition of capital.

Emmanuel does concede that the differences in standard of living between the rich and poor countries cannot be explained entirely by unequal exchange. Yet he still maintains that the basic mechanism by which value is transferred from the latter to the former is unequal exchange. Hence, all forms of international exploitation are but derivatives of the mechanism of unequal exchange.

Since the workers of the developed countries are, in his view, not only the initiators of the process leading to unequal exchange, but also its only real beneficiaries, while the losers are all consumers in the poor countries including capitalists there, the fundamental contradiction of international capitalism is, therefore, between the working class of the developed countries and society as a whole in the poor countries. Perhaps it is needless to emphasize what a false evaluation of the main front-lines of socio-political forces follows from such a conclusion.

Frantz Fanon

A hardly more realistic approach to the social sources of the transformation of world capitalism appears in the Fanonist concept[27] which equates the industrial working class as a whole with a labour aristocracy and looks for the world's revolutionary forces only among the poorest and most traditionalist strata of the peasantry in the periphery. Though Fanon's argument is based on a different theoretical premise and by no means relieves international capital of responsibility, it also reflects an inadmissible over-simplification concerning the sources of income and exploitation and the relationship between the political behaviour of classes and their income level.

The very fact of international exploitation and the recognition of the double burden of exploitation on the shoulders of the working population of the developing countries has induced a great many political thinkers — Marxists, Neo-Marxists and New Left theoreticians alike — to assume that the revolutionary forces capable of transforming the world capitalist system will come from the Third World. Their views, however, differ both in the assessment of the real or potential revolutionary forces that exist outside the Third World and in the assessment of Third World societies.

North–South
There are also a few pseudo-radicals or romantic anti-capitalists and naïve believers in the survival of traditional egalitarian societies who look upon the Third World as a more or less homogeneous society exploited by the uniform, exploiting bourgeois remainder of the world. Such a simplified world picture has, however, resurrected itself in the fashionable concept of North–South conflict. The latter, just like Emmanuel's theory, is concerned with the external relations of the two groups of countries — with the commodity, financial and technological flows between them. It overlooks the fact of the internal positions held by the capital of certain countries in the economies of others, as well as the different roles in international exploitation played by different classes within the countries concerned. By counterposing an undifferentiated South and an equally undifferentiated North, this approach can easily be manipulated and reduced to an apologia to conceal local class conflicts, to release domestic ruling classes from responsibility, and to gloss over economic imperialism.

Marxist Theories

The above survey of the main arguments on the international economy of conventional theory and the new schools of thought can be rightly criticized for being merely a sketch, involving considerable over-simplification and leaving out of account a number of significant authors as well as numerous important theoretical results and changes in view even on the part of those mentioned.[28] The same critique may apply to the following brief outline of the evolution of the Marxist schools. We cannot obviously deal with the general theory of Marxism or its main components: dialectical and historical materialism, political economy and scientific socialism. Nor can we even dwell on the details of Marxian views on the world economy. Moreover the Marxism of today differs in many respects from the Marxism of yesterday, both because of further theoretical progress and due to changes in historical reality.

It is even less feasible here to report on the contributions to the development of Marxist theory made by a great many theoreticians, past and present, belonging to European, Asian, African or Latin American nations, capitalist as well as socialist. Their views naturally differ in respect of various phenomena, processes and details of the capitalist world economy and its transformation.

We have to restrict ourselves here to the evolution of Marxist theory's concept of the world economy and its transformation, while disregarding not only details but also the differences in views of Marxist theoreticians. Nor can we touch on the scholastic question: who among all those calling themselves Marxists can indeed be correctly characterized as such?[29]

These limitations are inevitable, given the size of this study. But risky as it is, the following chapters at least reflect the author's personal views which he hopes embody in turn Marxist views.

Though a theory of the capitalist world economy was not elaborated by Karl Marx — nor indeed did he even write a chapter on international trade — his general theory of political economy has provided numerous pillars for it.[30] There are his theses on the most general laws of motion of capitalism as a system. There are his concrete remarks on the worldwide activities of capitalism, including the 'extra-national' aspects of the primitive accumulation process, the worldwide activity of merchant capital, and the specific non-equivalence of international exchange. Also relevant are his critical comments on the dogmas and illusions of classical economics as well as his political views about worldwide solidarity and united revolutionary action of the working classes of all countries as the motive force for the transformation of the world from the capitalist system into an advanced collective system, a world communist society, through the transitional stage of socialism.

Marx was primarily interested in analysing the most general laws of motion and inherent tendencies of the capitalist system in relation to other socio-economic systems, in its 'pure' form as a highly abstract model. The basis of empirical data which he used was confined to the national economies of a few European capitalist countries. The result was that certain important analytical and methodological questions were left open or ambiguous in his work. One such issue was what was the appropriate unit of analysis of capitalism.

As a consequence, many of Marx's followers, both in the past and today, take the national economy as the appropriate unit of analysis for granted. They conceive the processes of the world economy merely as external relationships between autonomous national units. And they forget about those notes of Marx which obviously contradict such an assumption, as well as the very fact of the internationalization process. At the other extreme other Marxists look upon capitalism as primarily a world system, neglecting the specificity of the internal processes within national units.

Another consequence of the ambiguity of the Marxian stance concerning the appropriate unit of analysis appears in the apparently contradictory interpretations among Marxists of how the law of value operates at the world market level.

Though practically all the main categories and conclusions of the Marxian political economy of capitalism (including price formation, money, accumulation, relative pauperization, crisis etc.) take on a more or less different meaning according to whether the national economy or the world economy is taken as the primary unit of analysis, this circumstance is mostly neglected when the empirical verification of these concepts and findings is attempted.

Perhaps the most debated question, which is also relevant to the issue of the unit of analysis, in the theory of Marx concerns the *locus* of transformation, namely Marx's prophecy that a proletarian revolution would take place in the most developed areas of capitalism. His personal expectations may or may not have been correct. In any case it is often forgotten that his views actually changed and Marx, towards the end of his life, did expect a revolution in Russia rather than in England. Nevertheless the question remains: does the assumption of an advanced state of capitalism as a precondition for revolution refer to a certain stage of the development of the system *in general* or to its development in a *specific* place, i.e. a particular country where capitalism is more advanced than elsewhere?

In addition, we ought to remember that capitalism both on the national and the world level has developed further since Marx's time and entered new stages which he could not have analysed in their mature forms. Indeed the next generation of Marxists, including Bukharin, Hilferding, Hobson, Kautsky, Lenin, Luxemburg, Trotsky,[31] and others, did analyse a new stage of capitalist development. This was characterized by among other things the international mobility of capital and the imperialist exploitation of colonies. This stage, called imperialism or monopoly capitalism by Lenin, has given an even greater significance to the question of the appropriate unit of analysis. It has also shown the importance and necessity for Marxist political economy of empirical studies of non-European parts of the world.

This latter point is an important one. Marxism was born in Europe. It bears certain birthmarks of European culture — the philosophical traditions of Rationalism, Darwinism, Hegelian dialectics, French utopian socialism, and British classical economics. And as we have just noted, the illustrative examples and concretely analysed cases in Marx's work were mainly, though not exclusively, European ones. This explains why its universal message, its applicability or adaptability to the non-European and less developed parts of the world, has understandably often been questioned.

Lenin's theory of imperialism[32] as monopoly capitalism obviously involves a world system approach, without denying, however, the national framework of some basic socio-economic processes in the developed countries of capitalism. His five characteristics of imperialism are partly related to the development of capitalism at a national level. These include the tendency to monopoly stemming from the further accumulation and centralization of national capital, and the rise of a domestic financial oligarchy. But Lenin's analysis also stresses the expansion of capitalism on a world level; in particular the dividing up of the world into economic spheres of interest shared out among the monopolies, and its division into politically and militarily controlled territories by the imperialist powers. The central fact of the international mobility and activity of capital connects the two levels of analysis and provides the key to understanding the development of the capitalist world economy as an organic system. In this way Lenin's approach resolves the one-sidedness of the question about the appropriate unit of analysis.

However, the ambiguous wording of this key factor — capital as an export, which refers to an exporting nation and its transactions — explains why the substance of Lenin's concept, namely the international separation of ownership and operation of capital (in particular the internationalization of the labour–capital antagonism) has often been misinterpreted or even missed in Marxist literature. Though Lenin's theory clearly pointed to the process of monopolization *cum* internationalization, and also to centre–periphery relations, both of which are related to the export of capital as the third characteristic of imperialism, many Marxists overemphasize either monopolization or internationalization, and some of them even question the empirically proven fact of the periphery's economic dependence.[33]

Lenin's short piece on imperialism, despite its richness of thought, was not followed by an elaboration of the political economy of global monopoly capitalism. For a long time even the economic functions of the dependent countries of the periphery remained as a general thesis without any detailed analysis of their implications for the development alternatives they faced. Nor were the changes that had taken place since Lenin's work analysed. This is one example of the grave consequences of the dogmatism that prevailed in Marxist circles for several decades. It probably also followed from objective historical circumstances which turned attention in the Soviet Union and later Eastern Europe primarily towards the national problems of developing a socialist system.

Lenin's theory of monopoly capitalist imperialism has given an answer, implicit rather than explicit, to the question of the appropriate unit of analysis by referring to the 'chain of imperialism' with its strong and weak 'links'. His analysis and political conclusions also showed how Marxism could be adapted to the circumstances of less developed countries like Tsarist Russia and her Asian territories. Nevertheless, these and related questions did not cease to be debated. This was so both because Lenin's views were not unanimously accepted by all Marxists at that time, and also because actual historical circumstances shed new light on the problem of world transformation.

Contrary to expectations, stemming perhaps also from Lenin's 'chain' concept of imperialism, the revolutionary chain reaction did not successfully unfold across the world after the First World War. Indeed it failed in precisely the most advanced countries of capitalism, and left behind a permanent revolutionary result in only one country. This fact and the consequent practical dilemma — what to do in that single country: build a national system of socialism or encourage a new global chain reaction of revolution — understandably sharpened the debate over the unit of analysis or, to be more exact, the unit of *action*. It led to a split between Leninists and Trotskyists. The failure of the chain reaction of revolutions in Europe and the subsequent stabilization of the capitalist system worldwide raised serious doubts about the correctness of a world-system approach. Some still insisted on its general application and the vision of an imminent world revolution; they suggested that Soviet power be used either as a means for exporting revolution (denying thereby the role of national forces) or as a means of developing industrial *capitalism* in Russia (denying thereby the role of socialist forces and their ability to start a socialist transformation in an underdeveloped semi-periphery country). In contrast, Lenin responded to the new situation in a more realistic way. Without forgetting the fact of a world capitalist system with its rules of the game and the existence of a single capitalist world market from which, as he stressed, 'we cannot escape', he urged and personally directed the Soviet Union's post-revolutionary efforts towards overcoming underdevelopment and starting a socialist transformation in his own country.

The realism of this programme was based on the recognition of two circumstances. First, the limitations on the Soviet Union as a result of the impact of, and threat posed by, world capitalism. Second, the opportunities in a huge country rich in potential resources, and in the particular circumstances of the level of development of productive forces in the world at that time, of going ahead with socialist development in a single country even before any worldwide revolutionary transformation.

It was, however, the very results of this programme, achieved by the Soviet Union mostly under circumstances of isolation from the capitalist world economy, that seemed to provide an empirical verification for the exclusive application of a national system approach in political economy and systems analysis. Ironically the achievements during the Stalin years — the elimination of mass unemployment, poverty and illiteracy, class privileges and exploitation, and rural misery; the restructuring of the economy by industrialization, national planning and the rise of R and D capacities; the great achievements in education, cultural life and social services etc. — gave an apparent validation to the emphasis in the dogmatic Marxism of the time on a national rather than an international approach.

After the Second World War, however, attention has increasingly turned again towards international relations and to the non-European parts of the globe. In addition, the breaking away of a few more countries, including Asian ones, from the world capitalist system put the problem of socialist development within a national or regional framework in a new context.

In the period of the Cold War, the complexity of the world transformation process was to a great extent reduced to a simple formula of antagonism between the imperialist states and their local agents on the one hand, and the socialist states with their natural or potential allies (the anti-colonial liberation movements) on the other. This reduction, even if it followed from historical conditions, did not help the subtle analysis of contradictory tendencies and complex phenomena.

Since the Cold War also prevented economic relations between the 'capitalist West' and 'communist East' from developing, the breaking away from the capitalist system took on the character of an isolation from the capitalist world market[34] and the autarchy of the individual national economies concerned and of their regional economic community. Again, the result was the neglect of the issue, how to develop a socialist system in countries which do participate in the world economy under the normal conditions of international economic relations. Another result was a certain over-emphasis on purely economic performance with great stress being laid on socialist countries trying on their own to catch up with the advanced capitalist countries and even to surpass them economically. This contributed to the prevalence of an economistic and primarily quantitative approach to socialist development.

Turning to the Third World, which Marxist analysis had tended to neglect, the anti-colonial liberation movements had seemed before the collapse of the colonial system to attack not only imperialist power structures but also capitalism itself. And the case of the few Asian countries where the success of the liberation movement had directly resulted in a socialist take-over, was thought to be a general precedent valid for all former colonies. Besides, the conditions of the Cold War made almost all socio-political phenomena in the Third World appear through the prism of the East–West confrontation and take on a more or less direct strategic, even military, importance.

All these circumstances undoubtedly held back — but, of course, cannot excuse the failings of — Marxist analysis of the actual realities of the world transformation process and its contradictions. Dogmatic prejudices and over-simplifications seemed to be verified for a while.

Since the late fifties false appearances have been destroyed by reality, its objective changes, and by science. And there grew up a subjective recognition of many former errors. Détente and more or less normalized economic relations between East and West led to the increasing participation of socialist countries in the worldwide division of labour and the world market. This made the contradictory interactions and complexities of the world transformation process sufficient to defeat the earlier, oversimplified and dogmatic visions. It became obvious that socialist development in a national framework or even in a community of nations is by no means a linear process of economic growth following in some almost automatic way from the elimination of private ownership over the main means of production. Nor can a ready-made recipe for socialist development be simply copied from the example of the pioneering socialist countries. It has also turned out that no single model can be applied to the post-colonial development of the Third World, and that decolonization does not necessarily mean independence to make real choices.

It is perhaps strange but understandable that before the world economic crisis in the 1970s, a kind of world system approach was applied only by a few ultra-leftist 'world revolutionaries', who also attacked the socialist countries, and by those many scholars involved in development studies, who explained the underdevelopment of the Third World in the context of the centre–periphery relations of the global capitalist economy. The latter rejected the special pleading and obviously ahistorical underdevelopment theories of conventional non-Marxist economists, with their concepts of a vicious circle of poverty, stagnant traditional societies and Rostowian stages of economic growth. It was clear that underdevelopment could not be explained without taking into account the historical context of world capitalist development.[35] By relating the underdevelopment of the periphery and the development of the centre to each other, the new radicals in development economics necessarily put the problematic of the socio-economic development of the advanced capitalist countries also in a world context (which the classical theory of imperialism and the classical explanation of the rise of the Western labour aristocracy had also done). Moreover, attempts were now made to explain the level of development and high incomes achieved in the advanced industrial countries in terms of the exploitation, by means of trade, of the underdeveloped countries. Nevertheless no consistent, theoretically convincing and historically verifiable conception of the appropriate unit of analysis of systems emerged and gained acceptance.

This situation, no doubt, arose partly because of certain weaknesses, a kind of infantile disorder, in Marxist development studies and dependency theory. They neglected, for example, the dialectics in the relationship between the parts and the whole, and between the external and internal factors in underdevelopment.

It was, perhaps, the recognition of the fact that social class relations crossed geographical frontiers and economic processes transcended national boundaries (not to mention the obvious lack of national economies in a considerable part of the world) that inspired Immanuel Wallerstein and others to develop their undoubtedly necessary but somehow biased *world systems approach*.[36] In this view the world economy and society constitute a single capitalist unit with an all-embracing division of labour and exchange between core states, the periphery and the semi-periphery, and accompanied by a multiplicity of separate political and cultural units, i.e. nation states. National economies do not exist, nor are societies really national. Even social classes are only 'classes of the world economy'.

Since the world capitalist system does not have a single political structure or world government, the surplus produced within the framework of the worldwide division of labour can be redistributed only via the market, which — according to Wallerstein[37] — is the *characteristica specifica* of capitalism. This capitalist world economy with its chains of commodity transactions crossing state boundaries (and being hardly different in this respect in 1500 and today) emerged in the 16th century, and since then has only shown a spatial growth, a geopolitical expansion, and a cyclical pattern over time, without any other stages of development.

The rise of the world market and an integrated division of labour on the one hand, and the simultaneous formation of strong nation states surrounded by other much weaker states on the other, has given the world system since the very beginning an unequal structure with an antagonistic contradiction between its core and periphery areas. This basically bi-polar system does, however, also have, in Wallerstein's view, a so-called semi-periphery which is defined as an intermediary stage, to be distinguished quantitatively rather than qualitatively from the latter. What actually determines the core, periphery or semi-periphery status of individual countries is, in the last analysis, the strength of their state power, which is the main weapon available to achieve a more favourable allocation of role and share of income in the integrated world economy. The very integration of the world market — i.e. the worldwide prevalence of exchange relations — makes *all* the participants in it and *all* social production relations and forms of exploitation substantially capitalist.

This picture of the world capitalist system and its history, despite the great many significant details and relations it reveals, makes the very dynamics of the system's development and its substantive historical turning-points disappear. It blurs the qualitative differences between the process (and stage) of primitive capital accumulation (i.e. the application of non-economic forms of coercion) and the developed capital accumulation process (whereby economic pressures compel 'free' labour to be deprived of its product). No longer is there a distinction to be seen between a dominant capitalist mode of production and subordinate, distorted but nevertheless pre-capitalist forms. No difference appears to exist between the development path of the core countries and that of the periphery. It leaves unanswered the question: what determines the strength of a nation state, which its more or less favourable role in the world economy depends on?

From the assumption that capitalism was born quite suddenly as a world economy and will die only as such, while throughout its span nation states will simply circulate between core, periphery or semi-periphery positions, it follows that peripheral and semi-peripheral states, no matter what social forces are behind them, can never break away from the global capitalist system but can achieve at best an improved position within it. In other words, a post-capitalist, socialist transformation cannot even start except at the world level. Its pre-condition is the rise of a world socialist government which replaces exchange relations by a worldwide system of planning allocation and distribution.

Wallerstein's denial that any national economy or society can exist, while accepting only that the political superstructure can have a national character, leads logically to the denial that a socialist transformation, let alone socialist development of an economy and society, can ever start within a national framework. It follows that no society currently characterized as socialist is in fact so.

How will such a world socialist government suddenly appear if the system as a whole remains capitalist until the latter comes into existence? Must one assume some all-embracing and synchronized world revolution? Or some shocking world catastrophe? Apart from these difficult questions, Wallerstein's approach seems to involve a certain limited interpretation of the dialectical relationship between the whole and its parts, and also between socio-economic and political processes. It assumes that the parts can be changed only by a change in the whole, but not the other way around. This means reducing dialectical interaction to a one-way process only. It also implies that in the capitalist system, while socio-economic relations are directly and exclusively shaped on a world level, they can be separated from the political superstructure established at a national level. Both assumptions imply far-reaching conclusions concerning the ways in which the world transformation process can take place.

Marxism, no doubt, is still very far from a general acceptance and consistent application of two, equally primary and dialectically inter-related units or levels of analysis, namely the world and national units. It still does not interpret the categories of political economy adequately on both these levels, in accordance with the double historical function of capitalism giving birth both to a world economy (but without an adequate corresponding global political superstructure) and to national units (in both a political and a socio-economic sense) in its core areas, while preventing the rise of truly national units in its periphery. Nevertheless the new thinking stemming from world-level analysis and the systematic correction or jettisoning of some old approaches seem to mark a new phase in the regeneration of Marxist thinking in these areas.

One example of those former paradigms, particularly prevalent in Eastern European Marxist textbooks until recently, is a simplified vision of the process of socialist transformation of the world. This vision, as already mentioned, practically reduced the development of world socialism to, firstly, an increase in the number of countries having chosen a socialist path and co-operating with each other outside the bounds of the capitalist world, and secondly, to the economic growth of these countries.

Many implications follow from this oversimplified view of reality. They concern such fundamental issues as the criteria of socialist transformation in individual countries, the internal laws of motion of existing socialist systems and the nature of their external relations, the very meaning of delinking or breaking away from world capitalism, the prospects for socialism in the Third World and in the West, the role of socialism in the emancipation of nations and in bringing about a new international order. All these issues have been raised afresh, in one way or another, by the empirical facts of reality, particularly by the crisis itself, and have become the subject of new discussions and thoughts.

As regards the nature, goals and current problematic of existing socialist states, most Marxists seem to agree now that these states are in no way nearing completion of a long historical process of constructing fully developed socialist societies. Nor are they anywhere near transition to a communist society. At best, they are only at the beginning or, perhaps, a certain intermediary phase of constructing socialism.[38] Indeed they may only be building a partially new, neither purely socialist nor capitalist system.[39] The development path of the socialist countries is also not seen any more as a model for imitation, let alone a single model,[40] and the lessons drawn from any one experience may only apply to others in widely different ways. It remains to be noted that there are still some conservative Marxist dogmatists who still believe in Stalin's theses, as well as others like Bettelheim[41] who deny completely the socialist character of development in socialist countries, including the October Revolution in Russia.

A few changes in Marxist thinking on development problems and what orientation to socialism may exist in the Third World have also to be recorded.

The eruption and consequences of the world economic crisis of the 1970s and 1980s have also put the assessment of the position and prospects of the Third World as well as Marxist development studies in a new light. A great many assumptions, more or less generally accepted theses and conclusions in the pre-crisis literature have now been questioned. An increasing divergence of views seems to have followed from the theoretical responses to the manifold, complex and controversial symptoms of the crisis. And there are signs of a new phase in development studies.[42]

The temporary success of the oil-exporting countries weakened for a while the earlier arguments about dependence, trade exploitation and the structural disadvantages of the developing countries' specialization in primary products. Moreover, the relative success of the handful of newly industrializing countries which were co-operating intensively with foreign, transnational capital, also seemed to undermine the former Marxist critiques of foreign direct investment and the redeployment of transnational corporations' activities to some Third World countries.

Then there were the serious difficulties, deadlocks and even, in some cases, about-turns and abortings in the socialist transformation of certain Third World countries and the rather poor economic performance of most of those developing countries which had apparently chosen a socialist orientation. Many Marxists as a result lost faith in the possibility of underdeveloped countries undertaking a socialist transformation before having achieved a fully fledged local capitalism. Some of them recalled the classical Marxian assumption (without bearing in mind its particular historical content and level of analysis) about the necessity for capitalism first to establish the material, social and cultural conditions required for socialism. Other Marxists even resorted to the conventional non-Marxist paradigms about foreign capital being a development agent; they reassessed the role and nature of imperialism and colonialism as well as the activities of the transnational corporations.[43] Contrary to both dependency theory and the historical facts, they assumed foreign capital could promote a full transformation of pre-capitalist societies (almost a kind of 'civilizing mission'). They also denied the net drain of surplus from the periphery and the disequalizing effects of the colonial international division of labour and the negative consequences of technology transferred by TNCs. These Marxists actually join with 'the commonplace Right', sharing also 'an anti-Third World tone', as Amin and Lipietz correctly note.[44] A few others also questioned the very concept of a centre–periphery dichotomy in the world capitalist system. They argued that the concepts of dependence and development distortions were biased in favour of the Third World and resulted in unjustifiable claims against the developed nations and incorrect economic policies.[45]

This swinging away from Marxist dependency theory and the idea that Third World countries could turn towards socialism, however, has not become a predominant feature of the new Marxist literature. The very development of the crisis itself, with its harmful effects not only on the non-oil exporting primary producing countries but also on the OPEC countries and NICs, has reinforced the main points of the Marxist critique. There is a renewed awareness of the validity of its arguments: the unequal structure of the international division of labour; the inherent disadvantages of specialization in primary production; the false or perverse nature of the kind of industrialization promoted by the redeployment activities of the TNCs; the regular loss of income as a result of the activities of these corporations; and the disguised forms and mechanisms (including transfer pricing) by which developing countries are exploited. The crisis has also inspired a more realistic and dialectical approach to the strategy of socialist transformation and independence, as well as to the problematic of North–South and East–West relations.

As a result of its positive response to the warning signs of reality and the defeat of dogmatism, Marxist research has made considerable progress since the late fifties. This is manifested in the increasing number of new publications on contemporary problems in the world economy, including its unexpected phenomena and recent changes. It is also to be seen in the new and open debates on numerous controversial questions which have to be theoretically answered. This progress, if it continues, promises to lead to the elaboration, within Marxist political economy, of a consistent and up-to-date theory of the world economy, a theory which is still missing or exists only in fragmentary form.

3. The World Economy: A Brief History

Problems in Periodizing History

The historical development of the capitalist world economy and its stages, if acknowledged at all,[46] can, of course, be described in widely different ways. It depends on one's interpretation of the determinant factors in development and the qualitative characteristics of international capitalist relations.

Even among Marxists who otherwise agree on how capitalism arose historically in Western Europe and who make a rather clear distinction between the classical (competitive) and monopolistic stages of capitalism, implicit or explicit disagreements appear in respect of the actual birth date of capitalism as a world economic system and its stages of development. Such disagreements flow from the obvious difficulties of conceptualizing the complex and contradictory processes of world history in any logical order and relating them to particular dates.

They also have differences of view as to the component forces and sources of cohesion in the world economy. The role of colonization and regular commodity exchange based on a structured division of labour among countries may be acknowledged in general. But the effects of the rise and fall of the colonial system on the capitalist world economy are viewed differently, and so are the forces which have shaped the division of labour. While the unequal relationship between the metropolitan, developed capitalist (imperialist) centre and its underdeveloped (colonized) periphery is almost unanimously stressed by all Marxists,[47] there is no consensus on how this centre–periphery relationship may have changed or what periods in its development can be distinguished.[48]

Capitalism has evolved unevenly on both a national and a world level. It has socialized, though it has been unable to complete, the reproduction process on the national level, and internationalized it on the world level. These historical tendencies have been in sharpening contradiction with the private appropriation of surplus value by capitalists and in contradiction, too, with the dominant, monopolistic position of certain nations compared to others. As a result, the stages of capitalist development within particular countries, even in the pioneer ones, have neither necessarily preceded nor perfectly coincided with the development stages of capitalism internationally. The decisive factors in the international development of capitalism, and hence in centre–periphery relations, have been the fundamental antagonism between labour and capital and the contradiction between the advancing socialization of productive forces and increasingly monopolistic relations of private appropriation within particular societies. But the international development of capitalism has also affected capitalist tendencies within national boundaries. As a consequence, uneven development has become a general law of capitalism. This makes any historical periodization of capitalist development not simply difficult but even contradictory.

The law of unequal and uneven development seems to have a far wider applicability and deeper content than the tendency noted by Lenin for changes in technological superiority to alter which countries held the leading position within the metropolitan centre. The law seems also to be a more universal characteristic of capitalism than the trend observed by several Marxist development theorists[49] today for the development gap between the centre and the periphery to widen. Its implications go far beyond the undoubted problems caused by the opening up of an international competence gap between forerunners and latecomers, which makes the development problems of the latter increasingly difficult as the economies of the former become ever more efficient in terms of productivity, infrastructure and human capital.[50] The law of uneven development works both within and between individual countries. It manifests itself not only in differences in the growth of productive forces but also in the variety of ways of forming social relations of production. Its operation on the world level causes shifts, both geographically and over time, in the normal stages of capitalist development; in fact it diverts practically all countries away from the theoretically predicted development path to be expected of the abstract model of capitalism. This is perhaps more obvious in the case of the periphery which has been the victim of a distorted capitalist development and an abortive process of primary, or primitive, capital accumulation. But it is no less demonstrable in the case of the centre where even if the normal stages of capitalist development followed one another as expected, each new stage as a rule did not unfold in the same country where the previous stage had reached its zenith.

Had capitalism developed only as a national system in each country, independently of each other and with no centre–periphery relationship, the linear concept of development would have applied and a classical sequence of stages could have been distinguished in each case. Alternatively, had capitalism developed only as a world system with its centre–periphery relationship fully determining the destiny of its parts, either no development stages could have been intelligibly distinguished or the historical stages of such a capitalist development, as embodied in a series of changes in centre–periphery relations, could have been traced back simply to shifts in non-economic relations of power between states. Reality, however, contradicts both cases.

What follows is that we have to compromise when trying to outline the historical process of the unfolding of the capitalist world economy in theoretical terms — as opposed merely to a chaotic chronological description.

We have to take into account both the stages through which national capitalisms have gone and the structural changes, related to the former, in centre–periphery relations.

The standard sequence of development stages of capitalism was realized in practice only in the centre, and then only in the centre as a whole and not necessarily in each of its constituent countries. The process starts with the stage of the primitive accumulation of capital, which the golden age of merchant capital paved the way for. It leads through industrial competitive, or classical, capitalism to the stages of monopoly capitalism and its most recent variant, namely one or another type of state monopoly capitalism. The historical evolution of relations between centre and periphery in the emerging capitalist world economy started with the period of mercantilist pillage (i.e. the forceful redistribution of wealth and development resources between countries) and long-distance trade in luxury goods and spices. It then proceeded during a long period of colonial dominance with its organized system of exploitation in production and trade together with the semi-colonial peripherization of those countries that remained formally independent but which had to adjust to the rise of a colonial division of labour. Only recently has the period of decolonization and neo-colonialism followed and the change-over of the world economy to a socio-politically mixed economy come about.

If we take both these sequences and their interaction into account, we may approach more realistically the actual history of the world system and understand more easily the background to its changes. Accordingly, we may distinguish four stages in the development of the capitalist world economy up to now. These stages, of course, contain several sub-stages as well as taking place within long-term, Kondratieff-type waves and short-term business cycles which contain the seeds of the crises which manifest themselves:[51]

1. The stage of mercantilism and early colonialism.
2. The stage of the rise of a colonial division of labour between the competitive, classical industrial capitalism of the centre and the colonized economies of the periphery adjusting to the demands of the centre.
3. The stage of monopoly capitalist empires, each with its own internal bilateral relations with its colonies and capital mobility, reinforcing the dichotomous pattern of the world economy.
4. The stage of multilateralizing international economic relations of state monopoly capitalism, which gives birth by means of redeployment and transnational corporations to a neo-colonial division of labour between the centre and the periphery, and deepening asymmetrical interdependencies within a global mixed economy.

A perfect periodization, especially if we try and tie it to dates, does not of course exist. Phenomena typical of a given period can be found in other periods. Regions with different endowments and heritages have developed at different times and with what might be called their own uniquely coloured characteristics. But the problem of the existence of such deviations must be the subject of a separate and thorough study of comparative economic history.

The First Two Stages

The first stage was a transition from more or less independent traditional societies, coming into contact with each other only in war or by means of external trade,[52] to the emergence of an international economy with structured relations of dependence. This development signified a historic turning-point not only for the rising centre of what later became the world economy (by providing the extra-national resources required for primitive capital accumulation), but also for many of those countries which were being turned into the periphery and whose socio-economic development was consequently being blocked or diverted.

Mercantilism was the era of the dominance and expanding activity of merchant capital, and it eventually paved the way for industrial capitalism. Colonialism, which only became a fully fledged, economically organized and effectively utilized system as late as the last decades of the 19th century, had existed much earlier, too. To distinguish that earlier form of colonization, we may call it mercantilist colonialism, though it did not necessarily coincide completely in time with the era of mercantilism in the metropolitan economies.

Early colonialism was already closely associated with the economic characteristics and laws of motion of evolving capitalism. West European society, whose representatives made their appearance as colonizers in the remotest parts of the world in the 15th and 16th centuries, was a society in a specific stage of development, experiencing a transformation greater than ever before. This was the era in which new social relations were germinating in the womb of feudalism, the period of emergent capital. At that time capital appeared on the scene still in its ancient form, as merchant capital. But soon it was to break up the framework within which it had come into being. Soon it would cause the disintegration of the traditional pre-capitalist mode of production which would give way to new relations which would enable it to go beyond the sphere of trade and penetrate the sphere of production and get control over it.

Primitive Capital Accumulation

This was the beginning of the primitive capital accumulation process. In it emergent capital reorganized society in accordance with its own interests with merciless rapidity. It reduced foreign people to slavery just as cruelly as it created its own social base: the class of people dispossessed of their rights, driven off their land, deprived of their means of production and forced to work in the appalling conditions of capitalist manufactories — the proletariat. This was the heyday of merchant capital in Western Europe when the instinct of the new society, the instinct of capitalism, was the hunt for surplus value — a hunt that was increasingly gaining ground within the old, disintegrating society. As production was still carried on on a feudal basis, the hunt for surplus value took the form of the acquisition of tangible money, gold. But to get rich by means of trade, to get hold of much more money, is possible only if the exchange is unequal and one partner steadily gains while the others lose. But an exchange which is regularly and lastingly unequal has limited possibilities within the bounds of a given country. So the activity of merchant capital had to be directed towards foreign countries from the very outset. Its ideology, mercantilism, in fact believes in foreign trade as the source of a country's enrichment. Mercantilist thinking sees commodity exports as the way to increase a nation's wealth. For commodity exports earn a surplus of gold and precious metals, provided the least possible amount, and preferably nothing, is spent on commodity imports.

These were the economic motives for the open cruelties, robbery and piracy of early capitalism.

The process of so-called primitive capital accumulation deprived producers of their means of production and hence created a 'free' class, the proletariat, confronted by the owners of the means of production (capital). This is what gave birth to capitalism. It was at one and the same time both an internal process leading to the rise of a capitalist nation state and capitalist national economy in the country concerned, and an external or international process resorting to extra-national sources of accumulation and leading to capital extending its exploitation over foreign countries. The two sides of the process, however, did not perfectly coincide in time. Since the primitive accumulation of capital involved both the forceful proletarianization of domestic producers by means of the application of non-economic force, and the equally coercive physical accumulation of capital in real money terms (precious metals) as a result of the foreign activities of merchants, the latter process partly historically preceded and prepared the ground for the former, and partly followed it.

The life-time of mercantilism was not the same internally as internationally. Merchant capital continued to play a decisive role in the external accumulation of capital, i.e. from extra-national sources, and also in starting the process of primitive accumulation abroad, even after the latter process had been accomplished in the mother country. It also served in the preparation and organization of the first international division of labour, which only fully unfolded in the second or the third stage of capitalist development — depending on the regions concerned. As a consequence, many phenomena typical of mercantilism — such as the worldwide activity of merchant capital, the various European trading companies, the intercontinental slave trade, and the introduction of colonial primary production, not to mention colonization itself — can be observed, albeit to a varying extent, in all of the first three stages of capitalism. It is therefore extremely difficult, even arbitrary, to draw a sharp division in time between the first and second stages. Wide differences appear both in the time-table of the processes in question, and their actual consequences, in the Asian, African, and American continents, and also within the latter. These differences followed partly from the different social patterns and development levels of the particular West European countries pursuing policies of conquest in different parts of the world, and partly from the substantial differences that existed between the various Asian, African, American (and also some European) societies which were conquered or at least dominated.

Nevertheless it is reasonable to make a distinction in theoretical terms and approximately rather than in precise order of time between the first and second stages, because the rise of industrial capitalism in the centre substantially modified the pattern of interests as well as the position and function of merchant capital.

Industrial Capitalism
In the second stage, once the industrial revolution is under way, the dominant capitalist interests are primarily those of productive capital; and they differ from the merchant capital of the pre-industrial revolution period. Merchant capital lost its primacy internally within each country. And as it became increasingly subordinated to productive and industrial capital, it had to adjust its activities internationally more and more to the needs of the former. This found one expression, among others, in the policy of trade liberalization. This so-called free trade was declared and imposed upon other countries, but was hardly practised by the leading industrial powers in their own markets. A second change that took place was a definite shift in the structure of international trade away from luxuries and precious metals towards those essential goods, mainly primary products, which metropolitan industrial capital now demanded.[53]

In this second stage, the relationship between the centre and the periphery already appeared largely as a production relation, i.e. a more or less organic and complementary division of labour between the industrial centre and the primary producing periphery.

However, certain regions were left out of this pattern. Others had to fulfil a specific, but different function for it. Thus Africa continued for a long time to contribute via the profits of the slave trade to the primary accumulation of merchant capital, as well as to the establishment of periphery production in the American continent as a result of supplying the labour force for the plantations there.

The development of the first colonial international division of labour was, therefore, only partial. But it is important to note that its rise heralded non-economic modes of violence against, or even the voluntary submission of, the periphery countries. For the subjection of the latter was not yet based upon relations of the international ownership of capital as the most fundamental social relations of production.

It was the international flow of commodities rather than capital, and the exploitation of the new periphery by merchant rather than productive capital, which were the dominant features distinguishing the period of *laissez-faire*, competitive capitalism from that of the subsequent monopoly capitalism and imperialism. It therefore involved a mercantilist type of colonial trade with the periphery, or only such free trade (itself largely the result of coercion) as promoted specialization in primary production.

Since an economy cannot simply be equated only with commodity exchange, the rise of the world economy can by no means be reduced simply to the fact of expanding trade relations between countries or continents. The first and second stages of the development of the world economy can, therefore, be interpreted as stages which prepared the way for, rather than realized, its full unfolding. That unfolding required not only its spatial extension worldwide but also, and primarily, the operation of an organic system.

Unless we conceive the capitalist world economy as merely the juxtaposition of separate national economic units, or just the sum of external economic contacts of the world's individual countries, we cannot miss a critical turning point in the unfolding of the world economy:[54] the appearance of foreign investment capital. From now on an external economic power operated as an internal factor in the economies of the periphery. For the first time there arose, as a result of capital export, international ownership relations crossing national frontiers.[55]

Before, however, discussing this third stage, let us summarize briefly the main consequences of the first two stages from the point of view of the transformation of the world into a global capitalist system, and its resulting inequalities and requirements for further transformation.

Centre–Periphery Relations Emerge

The first stage, i.e. the period of early colonialism and mercantilism, led, as we have seen, to unequal exchange and sheer plundering of foreign, mostly conquered, territories. It constituted an important part of the historical evolution of West European capitalism. It was also the beginning of world economic relations as well as the vehicle of the decline and distorted development of many non-European societies. Long distance trade in luxuries between countries and continents had of course existed long before this stage. But the role of mercantilism in preparing the way for the later rise of a capitalist world economy involved much more than the mere expansion of trade relations. It actually restructured the patterns of trade relations that already existed. It disrupted traditional patterns of living, production systems and sources of cohesion in the societies affected. It even transplanted institutions, religions, cultures and actual populations. New relations of domination were introduced or old ones reorganized. In general, if we disregard the marginal exceptions, we can say that since this stage of world capitalist development practically no society in the world has been able to go on living as before and follow its own former path of development.

Along with Western military and economic power which was manifested in the 'discovery', conquest and exploitation of 'new' lands and peoples, the Western spirit, which was really the spirit of a rising capitalism with its cruel rationalism, economism, individualism and hypocritical Christianity,[56] began to spread all over the world. This spirit and the West European languages, cultures and ideologies associated with it began to oppress and swallow up the rest of the world.

The Western bourgeoisie which was now on the ascendant made use of the ideology of anti-feudalism, anti-traditionalism, individual liberalism and nationalism, to weaken the ideologies of the opponents it encountered.

The second stage continued many of the actions launched by the first one. But it also added new elements to the process of the development of the capitalist world economy. International trade took on a more and more structured character. And the outlines of an international division of labour appeared. There were also a great many other changes in socio-political forces, ideologies, etc., both in the centre and in the periphery. These included the birth of an organized labour movement with its own anti-capitalist ideology, trade unions, political parties and international associations. As for the bourgeoisie, it began to lose its anti-feudal radicalism and progressiveness. Bourgeois nationalism shifted towards the late-comers of capitalist industrialization and the European periphery. Some former power centres — for example, Spain and Portugal — declined. And the first attempts were witnessed in the periphery to develop an imitative capitalism, particularly with the political success of anti-colonial liberation struggles in the American continent.

The differences in the actual position and development of the non-European continents as a whole, as well as within each of them, were not so wide during the first and second stages of capitalist development. It is therefore dangerous to generalize about the African, Asian and American cases. Nevertheless, we have to take this risk and refer to some of the differences between them.

Africa

The devastation caused by colonialism, its destructive impact on the social development already achieved in the past, and its paralysing effects on further progress were heaviest in Africa. This manifested itself in the destruction of prosperity and even sometimes of the very existence of the coastal city states which were based on trade with the outside world. Destruction showed itself primarily in the massive deportation of African slaves, the depopulation of the continent, the removal of its main productive force, human manpower, and the loosening or breaking up of the cohesive forces of local societies. The delay in the integration of Africa into the world economy was primarily caused by these destructive effects.

The deportation of slaves and the trade in other commodities like gold, silver and ivory not only caused the disintegration of African societies (though this was their primary effect), but also exercised an 'organizing' impact in the case of certain major, militarily stronger societies. Having already reached a certain level of economic development and social organization, and having built up some degree of state power, these societies were in a position to profit from the sale of natural resources or slaves captured as a result of subjugating other weaker tribes. The result was that certain traditional societies built on the common ownership and use of land shifted towards the Asiatic mode of production as a result of the increase in power and exploiting activity of tribal chiefs, military leaders and state officials.

The case of the North African countries was obviously different. This was because of the existence of 'archaic nations', a certain 'texture of national continuity', as Anouar Abdel-Malek calls it,[57] their inherited cultural–religious cohesion, ideological homogeneity and the tradition of centralized empires in countries such as Egypt. Also, Arab merchant capital was still playing a role in international and inter-continental trade.

Asia

In Asia, mercantilism, military conquest and the early colonialism of classical capitalism had perhaps less destructive consequences for the development of productive forces. But they did undermine the fossilized structures of these Oriental societies and brought about radical changes in the Asiatic mode of production. The European trading companies and military forces opened up Asian countries just as mercilessly as other territories to European trade and colonial penetration. By encouraging or forcing the expansion of trade relations, they actually gave a push to the development of local commodity production and even, for a while, local manufactures.

Latin America

In Latin America early colonialism and mercantilism appeared in a manner and with consequences different from those typical of the African or Asian cases. A form of feudalism, which had become outdated even in its native Iberian Peninsula, was imported. There was a massive extermination of the local population by means of seizing their lands and grabbing their gold and a forcing of the agrarian population to engage in mining under terrible conditions. During this period of early colonization, large-scale immigration from the Latin countries of Europe and massive imports of African slave labour took place.

The transplanted feudal institutions, however, did not result in a really feudal socio-economic system. Instead, Latin American feudalism was the product of the development of capitalism on a world level.[58] It had no roots in precolumbian local history and had nothing to do with a genuine pre-capitalist feudal system. Its origins were in one way similar to the European periphery of Eastern and Southern Europe, where the so-called second edition of feudalism[59] was already a part of the development of a periphery capitalism, as a capitalist reaction on the part of the feudal oligarchy to the challenge and needs of industrial capitalism in the West. Similar, too, to the case, of North America where the imported institution of slavery, with capitalist slave-owners, functioned in the service of a periphery capitalism which, again, was the product of the development of capitalism on a world level.

There is hardly any better proof of the discontinuity caused by colonialism in the endogenous and autonomous socio-economic development of the Third World, than the case of Latin America with its transplanted feudal institutions, immigrant ruling classes and imported African labour. Here is a graphic illustration of underdevelopment being distorted development.

In Latin America, unlike in Tropical Africa, a dualistic socio-economic structure[60] was already in the process of emerging during these stages of world capitalist development. It assumed a specific character in that leadership in the agrarian sector was held by a reactionary, conservative stratum of landowners who, owing to their origins and political ideas and world outlook, were rather closely attached to the metropolitan country. This stratum was getting rich by 'feudal' exploitation, or the exploitation of slave labour, and was increasingly engaged in more or less export-oriented capitalist production. In the towns leadership belonged to a more liberal social stratum less closely linked to the metropolitan country. It specialized in trade, the bureaucracy and military service, and reacted to changes in the outside world with more sensitivity. In economic terms, it was heavily dependent on the forging of foreign economic relations.

In other words, a variety of dualism emerged different from both the Asian and African patterns. In its Latin American version, the pre-capitalistic sector was assigned an important role in export production, and both its leading stratum as well as the exploited strata of African slaves and impoverished European and mulatto labourers consisted of immigrants. The leading stratum in the modern, urban sector, owing to its role as an intermediary and wider foreign contacts, showed more propensity for breaking away from the metropolitan country, and was ready to fight for its right to independent, national economic and political activity.

The successful anti-colonial struggle, however, in the countries of Latin America which gained political independence in the first part of the 19th century, did not result in an autonomous, autocentric national development of capitalism, nor did it bring about the rise of national industrial capitalism. Instead, and in a strange way, the elimination of colonial rule and the trade monopolies which had tied these countries to declining European colonial powers, opened up the road for an economically dependent periphery capitalism. Trade liberalization actually made it possible to adjust the production structure even more to the demands of foreign industrial capitalism than before and to develop a complementary, unequal division of labour with the industrialized countries of Europe and North America.

The post-independence development of Latin America in the 19th century was somewhat similar to the development of the various peripheral regions of Europe. In both, an outward-oriented, export enclave-led dependent economy developed as a result of the deliberate choice of the local ruling classes. The Latin American oligarchy, which constituted the main strata of what Frank called the lumpenbourgeoisie[61] — rural landlords, urban merchants, bankers etc. — managed to cater to their own interests contrary to those of the nation, in the same way as the landlord capitalists on the make in 18th century Eastern Europe, developed a primary product export enclave on the basis of cheap unskilled labour which was kept under pre-capitalist social conditions. The dominant classes in both cases made use of the consequent export revenues for imitative luxury consumption rather than productive investment in other sectors of the economy. Both were interested in export markets rather than the expansion of the domestic market, and local labour therefore represented only a cost factor rather than a potential source of effective demand. The introduction, preservation, or 'second edition' of pre-capitalist exploitation relations — slavery, peonage, or serfdom — seemed to fit perfectly the road of lumpendevelopment they had chosen.

This explains why the process of primitive accumulation was not carried through successfully in these regions. It also shows how peripheral capitalism with a disarticulated dualistic socio-economic structure and economic dependence, can result from the voluntary servility and selfish interests of local ruling classes under the effects of external economic factors.

The logic of history pointed to the possibility of the United States of America following a similar path of development, if the civil war between the South and the North had not stopped such a trend. Instead the plantation owners of the South were irremediably weakened by a victorious Northern industrial bourgeoisie whose economic interest prescribed the abolition of slavery, the formation of a real working class and the expansion, thereby, of the domestic market.

As we can see, in the first and second stages of the development of the capitalist world economy, the necessary preconditions for a periphery capitalism to emerge and for an unequal structure in the international division of labour to develop arose, in most cases, out of the non-economic violence (i.e. armed might) of the metropolitan powers, the direct intervention of colonial regimes or the voluntarily chosen economic policy of local ruling classes reacting to the economic effects and demands of the more developed centre of world capitalism.

In the third stage, however, these conditions were no longer absolutely inevitable though, as a matter of fact, in most cases they were maintained, strengthened or even introduced for the first time.

It is, perhaps, one of the paradoxes of modern imperialism from the late 19th century to the middle of the 20th century, that it retained and even expanded the colonial system despite the already existing possibility of making the periphery dependent and exploited without the institution of direct colonial rule. This explains why so many controversial interpretations of imperialism and the colonial system can be found even in progressive, anti-imperialist literature.[62]

Capital Mobility and the Third Stage

The third stage began with the rise of monopoly capitalism in the last third of the 19th century. It lasted until its transition into a state monopoly system of capitalism in the centre and the decolonization of the periphery, i.e. up to the 1940s and 1950s. The stage marked a decisive turning-point in the full unfolding of the capitalist world economy as an organic system. It involved the expansion and asymmetric internationalization of capital as a social relation of production — i.e. the separation of the ownership and activity of capital due to the appearance of the *foreign* ownership of capital which involved a social relation between foreign, absentee owners of capital and a local labour force.

This turning-point was soon followed by another political one, the 1917 Revolution in Russia. This ended for the first time the system-homogeneity of all parts of the world economy, which from now on became a kind of mixed-economy.

What is important about this third stage of capitalist development is that its crucial new characteristic (the extensive foreign ownership of capital) transformed the totality of production relations in the world economy into an organic system capable of functioning *without* non-economic forms of coercion. And the characteristics of the sphere of international circulation (trade and finance) became derivative from this fundamental fact.

The International Division of Labour

It is this turning-point which distinguishes the centuries-old epoch of the extra-national processes of primitive capital accumulation — the worldwide activity of merchant capital and the associated adjustment of the periphery enforced by military power and colonial administration or occasionally voluntarily undertaken by local ruling classes — from the new epoch in which the control of foreign monopoly capital over local economies became the primary mechanism ensuring the subordinate structural role of the periphery.

This new form of internationalization of the world economy by means of the foreign investment of capital has become the determining factor in the development of global exchange relations and the division of labour, as well as shaping international distribution. It has resulted in a much more integrated system than the earlier one, and it is a system which continues to expand through the further export of capital.[63]

In other words, a substantial change in the centre–periphery relationship ensued and the old commercial forms of colonial exploitation were replaced by the modern form of exploitation through productive capital and the complementary forms associated with it. The export of productive working capital — apart from capital taken abroad by emigrants — presupposes the separation of the ownership of capital from the activity of capital.[64]

A further condition of capital export of this kind is the regular and massive creation of surplus capital.[65] These conditions come into existence only at a higher level of capital accumulation and concentration, when the 'coupon clipping' capitalist becomes the characteristic figure of the economy.

Though the impact of the first two stages in the rise and development of capitalism in Western Europe had already been strong enough to stop or divert the autonomous development of those African, Asian and Latin American countries which were colonized or forced into economic contact with Europe, and an international development gap had begun to open up, it was nevertheless this third stage which decisively shaped centre–periphery relations. The result was accelerated dualism of development and under-development, both internationally and within the periphery countries.

This third stage resulted from the new monopolistic phase in the development of the capitalist mode of production as *laissez faire*, competitive capitalism was replaced by monopoly capitalism. The obvious signs of the new era became the scramble among the imperialist powers to acquire colonies, the redistribution among them of the occupied territories as a result of inter-imperialist wars, the dominant market position of giant monopolistic firms, the more and more intertwined interests of industrial and banking capital, and the increasing influence on government policy of this new, financial oligarchy. These developments could be seen both internationally and within each of the capitalist nations at the centre.

But perhaps the most decisive of all these new phenomena, and their culmination, was the penetration of working capital into the dependent territories. It was this factor which expanded and made more organic the international system of a colonial division of labour between metropolitan countries and their peripheries.

The international division of labour embraced both outright colonies as well as semi-colonial and other dependent countries, and was the expression of the historical development of capitalism at that time.

What factors determined the concrete structure and operation of this division of labour in that particular historical period? The answer lies in the internal conditions and external power relations characteristic of the countries of the developed sector of the world capitalist order and their position in the world economy.

Industrial development in the centre required an expanding market for manufactured goods. The purchasing power of the population at home with its still rather low income level could not provide a large and sufficiently expanding market. At the same time agricultural production in the European metropolitan countries was not able to ensure a sufficient food supply, nor to meet the demands of industry for raw materials. As a result, the European industrial countries, particularly Britain, became increasingly dependent on external sources of food and raw materials as well as on foreign markets. The more the internal laws of capital accumulation came into effect, the more the strange twins of domestic unemployment and the under-utilization of part of the accumulated capital, along with the tendency of the rate of profit to fall, became apparent concomitants of capitalist development. Thus, in addition to the acquisition of external sources of raw materials and foodstuffs and the conquest of foreign markets, an outward-oriented drain of idle surplus capital via foreign investments and a drain of surplus labour via emigration to the colonies became natural imperatives.

The increasingly powerful monopolies and militarily strengthened European states succeeded for a time in satisfying these needs. The way was marked by rivalry, hard bargaining, and cruel wars. The subjugated territories were balkanized, divided up and artificially differentiated in line with the different languages and cultures of the colonizing powers. But the process went on.

It was the satisfaction of the above needs that determined the economic functions of the subjugated territories. It was in this way that the colonies and semi-colonies became suppliers of minerals and agricultural raw materials to the metropolitan countries, sheltered markets for their industrial products, open fields of investment for their monopoly capital, and thereby their regular sources of income.

The international mobility of working capital also wrought radical changes in the structure and operation of international trade. While in the previous stages of development of a world capitalist economy, the debtor–creditor relationship was basically the consequence of the international exchange of commodities, the situation now turned into its precise opposite: international commodity exchange became more and more a function of the debtor–creditor relationship. And with this reversal of roles, both the content of this relationship and the conditions of international economic relations changed.

Reasons for the Export of Capital

The motives for the export of capital and foreign investment are often reduced in the literature to one or another partial aspect, usually the assumed greater profitability of exported investment capital. However, various other technological, social and political factors played a role and several other problems of the capitalist mode of production also required a solution.

One of the most important of them was the market problem, which is intimately connected with the capitalist character of the mode of production. The sharpening of the market problem within national boundaries tends to prompt a solution in the international realm. Only in this way can solutions apparently be found to the problems of under-utilization of productive capacities, the existence of idle capital, the ever replenishing army of the unemployed, and the cyclically accumulating stock of unsold goods.

The solution seems to lie in capital export, and primarily the export of working capital. This exerts a more long-lasting income-generating and market-expanding effect than loan capital. And its decisive impact on production structures also thereby shapes the international division of labour and specialization.

The utilization of idle surplus capital by investment overseas is another important motivation for capital export. Like the market problem, it reflects the natural process of increase in the productive forces and the capitalist framework of the process. The regular formation of capital surpluses follows from the limits to profitable investment opportunities domestically, or to be more exact, the limits on investment opportunities promising a certain minimum rate of profit within a defined period of time. This relative capital surplus, the phenomenon of over-saving and under-investment, is one of the most obvious manifestations, alongside over-production and under-consumption, of the contradictions of the capitalist system.

The process of investing excess capital abroad is of course closely connected with a further and exclusively social aspect of capital export, namely the profit motive. More precisely, capital export is also motivated by international differences in the rates of profit and the wider opportunities, under given business conditions, for making investments abroad.

Differences in the level of profit rates as well as the relatively wide range of investment opportunities have a variety of causes.

Besides these basic motivations of capital export, there are others which are also connected with the aim of a higher or safer realization of total capital. One of the motives for capital export may relate to the raw material basis required by the capitalist system's reproduction. The ongoing growth of the productive forces sooner or later demands that domestic resources be complemented by foreign ones. The efforts of monopoly capital are often aimed at taking possession of these foreign resources. How acute is the need to do so in the short term depends on the metropolitan country's own richness in natural resources, its policy on resource use, the efficiency of its technology and military considerations.

Another motive for capital export may be connected with the labour component of reproduction. Transferring certain elements of the reproduction process abroad by means of capital export makes it possible to exploit cheaper and for the most part unorganized foreign labour. The relative wage differences,[66] i.e. the fact of a wider gap in the level of wages than in the level of productivity, has been an important factor motivating foreign investment in less developed economies.

A further motive for capital export has to do with the technological and scientific basis of reproduction, the technologies applied and the research and development capacities ensuring knowledge of new techniques as well as product development. Foreign investment can lead to easier access to, or even effective control over, the technologies of a rival economy. Alternatively, foreign investment may become necessary because the application of new technology requires an expanding market and international co-operation.

Consequent Contradictions

Contradictions, however, appear from the very fact that the export of working capital separates ownership from the functioning of capital. The prevailing pattern of asymmetries all contribute to the inherent tendency to disequilibrium of the capitalist world economy.

Capital export is, on the one hand, a means of financing an export surplus, while, on the other, it also has its own specific objective: the acquisition of super profit. While the former function tends to expand the market and restore, at least temporarily, the equilibrium of international trade, the latter function tends to restrict the market and upset the equilibrium. While capital export ensures a safe foreign market, it reduces the propensity in the capital-exporting country to invest for the purposes of greater efficiency and competitiveness; on the other hand, in the capital-importing country it contributes to the expansion of production and technological development, and may make that market more competitive and less safe.

The contradictions between the various functions of capital export are not confined to these market-expanding and market-contracting effects, but can be found in other aspects as well. For example, the initial reduction in excess capital by means of exporting it may, if the subsequent profits from overseas are repatriated, actually contribute to a further increase in excess capital in the metropole. Not to mention that the banking channels created to facilitate capital export, can be used for an opposite flow of money, too. The international banking system makes it possible for idle local capital in the underdeveloped periphery, and the accumulated savings of its élite, to find its way into the banks of the capital-exporting countries at the centre, thereby reinforcing the periphery's need to import capital.

It is precisely an analysis of the contradiction between the two basic functions of capital export which offers the greatest help in understanding the direction of development of the capitalist world economy, the international division of labour and its effects on the position of the periphery. In other words, there is a contradiction between commodity and money relations resulting from capital export, i.e. a contradiction between exchange relations and debtor–creditor relations. This is at the same time closely related to the much-debated problem of what relationship exists between the export of commodities and capital export in the contemporary world economy.

The profit-earning function of capital export, i.e. the regular repatriation of investment incomes to the capital-exporting countries, limits the resources for accumulation of the capital-importing countries. So their growth potentials and the expansion of their purchasing power are also held back. If, as a countervailing measure in order to keep up the otherwise declining commodity-absorptive capacity of these countries, the influx of capital from the creditor countries continues to increase, but in an asymmetric pattern (i.e. without reciprocity in the flows of capital and income between the two sets of countries), then, as a result, the debtor–creditor relationship deepens and the imbalance in financial relations worsens.

An asymmetrically increasing capital inflow may give rise to cumulative indebtedness. This will be manifested partly in an explicit form (namely, an increase in the debt burden), and partly in an implicit form (an increase in foreign capital assets). It is hardly necessary to emphasize the consequences of this for the balance of payments and national currency of the debtor country. The consequences also make themselves felt in the harsher conditions then imposed for acquiring new foreign capital.

In principle, the disequilibrium in the trade and financial systems of a world economy in which the capital of the industrial centre operates also in the primary producing periphery, could be eliminated only if the terms of trade for the latter systematically improve. For this would then make up for the effect of profit repatriation on the periphery country's capacity to absorb industrial products from the centre. In short, it would ensure an equivalent growth of markets in both segments of the world economy. But such a trend in the terms of trade has not prevailed. Except for a few short periods, there has been, instead, a regular deterioration of the terms of trade of the primary producing periphery countries, which amounts to a characteristic of the capitalist world economy.

Specialization in primary production in the periphery combined with a monopoly of manufacturing industry in the centre has meant two poles in the world economy between which it is impossible, as recent economic history has shown so clearly, to bring about anything but an increasing disequilibrium.

What clearly follows from the above is that the role and significance of capital export can by no means be appraised simply on the basis of the statistical figures for amounts of capital transferred, the year-on-year changes in the volume of capital export. Account must also be taken of the direct and indirect role of the capital already exported and operating in the importing country. In contrast to commodity exports, or even to the export of capital as a commodity (i.e. loan capital), the export of working capital has lasting and cumulative effects. The consumption or utilization of exported capital results not in its disappearance, but, as a rule, its growing perpetuation. To ignore this essential difference between the nature of exports of working capital and commodity exports is to neglect capital as a social production relation.

The export of working capital has played a role in shaping the structure of the world economy and the economies constituting its component parts. It has launched patterns of export production in many periphery countries, which have transformed both national and international economic structures. Its distortion of production towards an export orientation has influenced the transfer of technologies, the processes of integration, monetary relations, and influenced economic policy decisions and development strategies.

The export of working capital also demonstrates the internationalization of capital as a production relation and is therefore, by its very nature, the form *par excellence* and vehicle for advancing the internationalization of production on a capitalist basis.

The Consequences of Monopoly Capitalism for the Periphery

This third stage in capitalist history has been the period in which the periphery of the capitalist world economy has become a qualitatively unique sector consisting of countries with substantially similar features, development problems and world economic position. And this is in spite of the differences that exist between individual periphery countries in the extent and forms of their structural adjustment to the needs of the centre.

From the point of view of the basic causes of the developing under-development of the periphery, it is only of secondary importance when exactly the socio-economic structures corresponding to the above-mentioned functions of capital export came into being in the various regions. Also of secondary importance is the question of within what constitutional framework this structure came into existence, whether it was as a colony, a protectorate, a mandated territory, or a formally independent state. The latter question is, of course, important politically, from the viewpoint of the sufferings of the people in the countries affected.

Differences in timing and differences in the actual role of local forces are responsible for how long the system, with its achievements and accumulating deficiencies, survived before becoming politically obsolete. These features also determined what counter-forces evolved in the system and how soon conditions became mature enough for a transformation to the subsequent neo-colonial period.

The political, administrative and military structure of colonialism, though far from being the most decisive aspect, also affected the further development of the periphery countries. The colonizers balkanized whole continents and regions by artificially designating the boundaries of their colonies. This had a profound impact on the future framework of their national economies and influenced the ethnic and social structures of their populations as a result of imposing upon them different foreign languages and cultures.

But in addition to the impact of such non-economic power structures, periphery relations have developed via the penetration of foreign monopoly capital shaping and adjusting the structure of the economy to the requirements of the international division of labour.

Foreign private capital, to take one example first, penetrated sheltered territories and built up or took over the key export sectors. The cause may have been the deliberate economic policy of the metropolitan state or its colonial administration, or merely the impact of the free play of market forces. But the result was always export-oriented agrarian monoculture and mineral production.

The narrowness of the domestic market, coupled with the strong demand-inducing effects of the world market, has justified from the very outset an export-oriented economy. Moreover this economy took a particular form. The external demand stimulated the production of minerals and agricultural products. Qualified local labour was in short supply. The import from overseas countries of machinery would have been very expensive. The result, therefore, was an agricultural system with low capital intensity and operated by cheap unskilled labour. And side by side with this, there were mineral extractive industries which were only more capital-intensive relative to colonial agriculture. These were the priorities for colonial investment. The need for marketing manufactured goods imported from the metropolitan country worked in the same direction.

The direct investment of foreign capital in the productive sectors and the commercial and financial spheres controlling these sectors, resulted in the disruption and further decline of the old, less developed local modes of production. These changes represented a new impulse to social transformation. This transformation, however, was not only more painful than in the countries where the internal forces of capitalism had played a dominant role, but, under the prevailing circumstances, was also doomed to failure.

As a consequence of the privileged, monopolistic position of metropolitan capital *vis-à-vis* any local or outside rivals in the colonized periphery, competition was practically eliminated, technological development impeded, and investment policy directly subordinated to the interests of the metropolitan economy.

A still more serious consequence was the fact that the leading positions in the economy, the commanding heights, were seized by foreign capital and foreign personnel. As a result, the sphere of national decision-making was confined, even where constitutional independence was preserved, to fields of secondary importance.

Equally serious were the consequences of a regular siphoning off of a substantial part of investment income and, parallel to that, a reinvestment of it, which constituted an increase in foreign capital assets, paving the way in turn for further income drains.[67] These withdrawals of income from investments can take place in a variety of forms of a mostly uncontrollable kind and through the most diverse channels. This explains the recurring balance of payments deficits of the periphery countries concerned.

However, the gravest and most decisive consequence of the direct investment of foreign monopoly capital, with its bias towards primary producing export enclaves, has been the disintegration and distortion of each peripheral country's economic and social structure. This manifests itself in the sectoral structure of the economy (the predominance of primary-producing enclaves), and also in sectoral and regional dualism. This is the peculiar symbiosis of two principal socio-economic sectors, each embodying a different mode of production, and one dominating the other.

The sectoral distortions and sectoral-cum-regional dualism restrain the expansion of the domestic market. They impede the spread of linkages between the different productive branches. And they perpetuate the problems of both unemployment and the shortage of skilled labour.[68]

All these various consequences cannot, of course, be indiscriminately generalized and applied without exception to all cases.[69] Nevertheless subordination, the drain of income and the structural distortions may be regarded as the natural effects of the international mobility of capital in an asymmetrical pattern (i.e. a large-scale one-way transfer of working capital by monopolistic companies). In principle, an inflow of investment capital ought to be able to open up unutilized sources of income, provide employment opportunities and transplant more advanced technologies and production methods. However, under the actual conditions of the capitalist world economy, these positive effects have been outstripped by the negative ones.

The colonial pattern of the international division of labour, in terms of which the production structures of the periphery have been finally shaped by the inflow of foreign investment capital, has achieved an expanding flow of commodities between the metropolitan centre and its periphery. Spontaneous external market forces of supply and demand have from the very outset determined the direction of economic activities and investments to which even local capitalist entrepreneurs and farmers have been compelled to conform. Thus in the development of monocultural export production and the sectors serving it, an active part has been played not only by foreign but also, in certain fields, by indigenous entrepreneurs and even small commodity producers.

The factors which caused the distortion of the periphery's economic structures and gave rise to the outward-orientation of a part of the economy and its isolation from the rest of the economy, soon became a cumulative process. The overwhelming predominance of foreign capital largely strangled local capital and prevented it from engaging in independent and competitive activity. The cumulative economic process which had been set in motion tended to swallow up all local economic activities that deviated from its own direction. Attempts at creating a national manufacturing industry were a notable casualty of this tendency. At the same time, in the wake of the spontaneous conforming to the interests of foreign capital, there sprang up as its appendages and subservient agents various secondary types of domestic capital. This so-called comprador capital or comprador bourgeoisie[70] comprised strata in the local society which were directly interested in co-operating with foreign capital.

Trade relations between the developed industrial countries and their primary-producing satellites have increased the raw-material exporting character of the latter and distorted their internal economic and social structures. The growth of the export-oriented sector and the expansion of the infrastructural and institutional network serving it, have increasingly diverted resources away from production for the satisfaction of the local population's basic needs and the infrastructure necessary to meet them.

The narrow export structure of periphery countries, with commodity production often assuming a more or less one-crop (monocultural) orientation, has been accompanied by the increasing propensity of their economies to import. The result is a heavy trade imbalance. This causes an additional regular loss of income, in addition to the repatriation of profits.

This income drain is rooted in the violation of the principle of equivalent or equal exchange.[71] This can be attributed both to the monopolistic or oligopolistic character of the market, and even more importantly to the inequalities in productivity and the structures themselves.[72] Trade between partners who are unequal in respect of their marketing and structural power may increase those inequalities and itself become a factor contributing to a widening of the development gap between nations.

The bilateral flows of capital and commodities in the colonial division of labour were to varying degrees complemented by parallel movements of human resources. This could be seen in the emigration of surplus labour from the developed capitalist countries to the colonies, especially in times of serious crisis or following wars. There was also the export of skilled labour, technicians, foremen and administrative personnel required by investments in the periphery, not to speak of the colonial administration's personnel and the army. On the other hand, there was also often a movement of human resources in the opposite direction as cheap, unskilled labour from the periphery was shipped to the developed economies.

In the peripheries, the better paid jobs were monopolized for the most part by European expatriates. This was owing to the flow of labour, more particularly white-collar workers and skilled labour, from the metropolitan countries.

Local labour was mostly needed for manual work in the plantations, mines, and services. It tended to be frozen into the cheap, unskilled categories. Since the quality of labour had hardly any chance to improve, and public education failed to develop appropriately, the shortage of skilled labour continued to exist side by side with an abundance and over-supply of cheap, unskilled labour. This dualism also played an important part in the operation of periphery economies.

The unfolding of this organic world economic system of capitalism, with its monopolistic one-sided internationalization of social relations of production and unequally structured division of labour between centre and periphery affected not only the periphery, but also the socio-economic and political development of the centre itself.

The internal tensions and social conflicts in the countries of the centre sharpened. This was due to the monopolization process stemming from the ongoing centralization and concentration of capital in fewer and fewer hands. It also resulted from the increasing separation of functioning capital and its ownership, of the active manager and the passive owner of capital. And with further proletarianization swallowing up formerly independent strata, the income gap between the working and capitalist classes widened. On the other hand, the increased economic utilization of the periphery generated income and benefits which made it possible for the metropolitan countries to mitigate domestic tensions by relatively privileging the upper stratum of the working class. This creation of a labour aristocracy is one of the reasons for the change in the revolutionary energies in the centre and the global shift in the geographical *loci* of revolutions in general.

The possession of colonies or semi-colonies ensured important resources for the economic growth and military power of the metropolitan countries concerned and also security for the external activities of their private capital. This explains the hunger for colonies which afflicted the late-comers in the sharpening rivalry between the countries of the centre, the end result of which was imperialist wars and, ultimately, the First World War.

On the other hand, the possession of an empire with protected markets and investment spheres from which outside rivals were excluded, reduced competition. But competition was the very engine of technological progress. So in one way the possession of colonies actually discouraged the development of productive forces in the metropolitan countries, as the case of Britain clearly shows. This effect also contributed, in part, to the shift, within the centre, in terms of which powers held the leading positions.

This third stage in the development of the capitalist world economy seems to be not only the first, but also the *last*, period in which the inherent tendencies of capitalism as a socio-economic system developing both on a national and a world level could manifest themselves more or less in their fullness and without being substantially disturbed by exogenous factors. All its internal antagonisms and dialectical contradictions — such as the labour–capital antagonism, the centre–periphery dichotomy and the contradiction between national and international development — came to the surface. They appeared eventually in their full complexity and produced deep crises and explosions in the system — wars between imperialist powers, anti-capitalistic revolutions, and national liberation revolts.

The culmination of these contradictions of the system led to changes in which metropolitan countries held the leading positions in the system. The socio-economic structures of particular countries were also changed. But there were far more radical changes. There was the rise of socialist regimes, particularly the Soviet Union. The liberation of certain colonies began a chain-reaction towards the collapse of the colonial empires. And there were the diverse reactions of the ruling classes in the centre to the crisis and to the challenge of socialist and national liberation movements — fascism on the one hand, a reformed welfare capitalism on the other. All these changes obviously shaped the circumstances for the next stage.

However, it should not be forgotten that even the normal evolution of the capitalist mode of production brings about considerable changes preparing the way for new stages in the development of the world economy. An undoubtedly new phase of internationalization and integration of the world economy has been opened up by the scientific and technological revolutions of the 20th century. This has facilitated a concomitant further internationalization of productive forces and deepening global interdependency. The process of transnationalization which has forged ahead with the mushrooming of transnational corporations since the Second World War is the most visible demonstration of this internationalization. And we must not ignore the impact of the new socialist economies which first delinked from, and recently began to relink again, with the world economy.

This new fourth phase shows considerable modifications, also, in the motives and patterns of capital export and foreign investments.

4.   Global Capitalism Since World War Two

A Single Stage?

The Second World War was itself a consequence of the crisis and heralded a necessary modification in the operation of the capitalist system. The fascist attempts of the 1930s to solve the crisis and organize a new order challenged all democratic forces — bourgeois liberal, patriotic and socialist alike. Following the victory of an alliance between capitalist states, the Soviet Union and local resistance forces, a great many substantial changes have taken place in the world economy and world politics. It is not necessary to discuss them in detail here. Clearly, a new stage has opened up, even if several of the new phenomena actually had their roots in the previous stage, or appeared only in a later phase of the post-war period.

What seems to be questionable, however, is whether the past four decades since the Second World War can in fact be taken as a single stage in the evolution of the world economy. Consider some of the radical changes and turning-points which have taken place in this long period:

★ The change from high energy- and raw-material consuming, environment-polluting technologies in the advanced countries to energy- and material-saving, environment-protecting ones as a result of the energy crisis and the recognition of ecological problems.

★ The rise, more or less in tandem with the latter, of yet another revolution in science and technology, following the previous one which had started during or just after the Second World War.

★ The eruption of a world economic crisis in the 1970s, which ended the former relative stability of the world market and international monetary system. The crisis induced a sharper competition and prompted a resort to state intervention in the fields of export promotion and protectionist measures. Structural roles in the world economy were to some extent redistributed. At the same time the increasing inadequacy of a purely national framework in the regulation of economic processes was demonstrated.

★ A new recognition of the global problems of humankind. This arose partly out of fears of depletion of the world's resources and consequent resource scarcity. As the first reports of the Club of Rome suggested, this possibly heralded the beginning of a new era in the world economy. Another dimension was a new awareness of the absurdity of the nuclear arms race and East–West hostility, which increasingly threatened the very survival of humankind, and which as a result put on the agenda the process of détente in order to end the Cold War.

★ The end of the Iron Curtain isolation of the East European socialist countries, as well as China, from the rest of the world. Some degree of relinking of their economies with the world economy began. This brought about some new features in the world economy as a result of the relative normalization of East–West relations, the development of East–South relations, and the new policy of *glasnost* in most of these countries.

★ The transition from the almost unchallenged economic and technological hegemony of the United States in the immediate post-war world to a period where the US is trying to counter the challenge of Japan and the European Economic Community, with projects like the SDI (Strategic Defence Initiative) programme.

★ The shift in the centre of gravity of the world economy from the developed North Atlantic zone which was dominant in the first post-war decades to the Pacific Rim which includes some newly industrialized South East Asian countries as well as Japan and the Western seaboard of the United States.

★ A certain crisis in the post-war system of Keynesian economic intervention by the state, welfare measures and state monopoly institutions in the developed capitalist countries since the 1970s. This paved the way for a monetarist counter-revolution and neo-liberal, ostensibly non-interventionist economic management policies.

★ The acceleration of the process of internal differentiation and polarization in the Third World. Since the late 1960s a relatively and (as it turned out) temporarily privileged group of countries, namely the major OPEC oil exporters, took advantage of the oil price explosion. And secondly, there has been the success, within the limits of underdevelopment, of a few newly industrialized countries which have adjusted to the new conditions and requirements of the world economy. On the other hand, there has been the further cumulative deterioration of the position of most Third World countries, stricken by mass poverty, epidemics, illiteracy, famine, and a development deadlock and debt crisis.

Such substantial changes in the post-war development of the world economy suggest the existence of more than one stage within the period of the last four decades. However, despite these changes, the period from the Second World War to the present day will be treated as one single stage. This is because the changes mentioned do not seem to contradict those fundamental characteristics on the basis of which this whole post-war period can be distinguished from the pre-war one. The whole period can be described as a stage of mainly military-biased scientific and technological revolution and state monopoly capitalism in the capitalist centre, neo-colonialism in the periphery, transnationalization and global interdependency, and an unregulated mixed world economy.

The above changes may be usefully interpreted instead as dividing this fourth stage of global capitalist development into sub-periods rather than opening a really new stage. One can argue, for example, that the recent wave of scientific and technological advances are closely linked with some of the other changes. Or that the change-over to energy- and resource-saving technologies is not just limited to certain fields and countries only, and not substantially reducing the on-going mass squandering of non-renewable natural resources, but is rather the outcome of those very modifications in world economic structures and power relations which characterize this post-war stage.

Similarly, the current global crisis of the world economy is a culmination of its own lasting fundamental contradictions and imbalances and its centre–periphery relations. But it also stems from those very structural and institutional changes which started in the first decades after the war, such as changes in capital exports, investment patterns, the division of labour, the redeployment process promoted by TNCs, the international arms race, the rise of a consumer society, and so on. Further, the world economy had already become a mixed economy when, after the war, several countries started on a socialist transformation. In the end, the isolation of these countries turned out to be untenable in the light of the growing internationalization of science and technology, communications and the reproduction process itself. It also proved counter-productive for those outside forces which had imposed such isolation on them in the first place.

As for the arms race, it started soon after the Second World War. The reasons included the rise in the number of socialist regimes and the hostile reaction to them of the developed capitalist powers. The two groups of countries took opposing views of the anti-colonial movements and new revolutionary forces in the Third World. The chronic tensions, military conflicts and regional wars in the Third World took place, as a result, in the context of global power tensions. The military–industrial complex developed a vested interest in the arms business and the army began to influence politics. Unfortunately, these tendencies have not yet been stopped. The Cold War is still with us, despite the recognition of its absurdity and the recent disarmament initiatives made by the USSR.

The ecological problem, also, has not been solved. Despite new technologies and counter-measures, environmental pollution and the wasteful management of resources continue.

Nor has the international development gap and underdevelopment syndrome disappeared. Indeed it has simply become more visible with post-war decolonization. True, the Third World is more differentiated than before and a few countries have managed to achieve a spectacular growth in industrial production and exports. But the success of these countries has only been won at considerable socio-political cost. Nor can it be repeated by all developing countries since it was based on the modifications in the international division of labour and business policies of the transnational corporations which this small number of countries were able to adjust to and take advantage of in the 1950s and 1960s. But these new features of the fourth stage of world economic development do not offer comparable opportunities to Third World countries as a whole.

As for those changes mentioned above which have proved to be temporary, perhaps the product of business cycles only, such as inflation or shifts in the relative economic and technological power of various countries at the centre, they do not imply any departure from the general trends of capitalism. They certainly cannot, therefore, be regarded as radical turning-points in the development of international capitalism, thereby distinguishing a new stage in its history. A certain crisis of the welfare state and Keynesian state intervention has certainly taken place. But the recent monetarist counter-revolution and neo-liberal rhetoric by no means proves the end of the state monopoly stage of capitalism. It does not even imply a substantial reduction in the economic role of the state, particularly when neo-liberalism is combined with state protectionism in trade, militarization, and aggressive monetary policies.

So let us not dwell further on arguments for or against the unified character of the current fourth stage in world economic history. Instead let us sum up briefly the most important features of this four-decade-long period since the Second World War and the basic changes characterizing it.

Key Changes in the World Economy

The world capitalist system lost its monolithic character in the world after 1917, with the survival of the first socialist state. However, due to the rather isolated development of the Soviet economy in the first decades after the Revolution, the operation of the capitalist world economy was not immediately substantially affected. The political effects were, of course, considerable, particularly in Europe, and explain a lot of the changes in the behaviour of local socio-political forces.[73]

The most obvious modification of the world economy after the Second World War, and particularly once there was a certain normalization of East–West economic relations in the 1970s,[74] was that the world economy which had been established, and was still dominated, by capitalism lost its simple, normal dichotomy between centre and periphery. It now became a tripartite system, a sort of mixed economy, with the participation of a number of socialist regimes.

In other words, the rise of new socialist regimes has had a double effect. On the one hand, it has affected indirectly the operation and structure of the world economy. On the other hand, the fact that the process of socialist transformation and development only started in a part of the world, in countries which were themselves economically less developed than those of the centre, has, under the conditions of a predominantly capitalist world economy, brought about contradictions in the socialist transformation process itself.[75]

A no less significant and far-reaching change in the world economy has followed from the collapse of the colonial system. This has undermined the former institutional basis and bilateral mechanisms of centre–periphery relations. The collapse resulted primarily from the successful struggles of national liberation movements after the war and changes in international power relations. Decolonization, however, did also reflect, at least in its later stages, changes in the interests of the leading capitalist groups. Shifts in the colonial pattern and the mechanisms of the international division of labour were therefore called for.

These disturbances in the colonial division of labour follow not only from its built-in imbalances and from changes in the relative power of states, but also from the emergence of a new pattern in the division of labour. As with all economic phenomena, these changes and disturbances in the international division of labour have a material–technological and socio-political background. They include factors which are effective in very different time dimensions.

The structural modification of the international division of labour, along with shifts in the pattern of international capital mobility, has been connected with substantial changes both in productive forces and social relations of production in the developed capitalist centre itself.

A New Scientific and Technological Revolution

Of all the changes that have taken place in the productive forces within the developed capitalist centre of the world economy, mention must be made, first of all, of the scientific and technological revolution which has leapt forward again in the capitalist centre. Of course it has done so in a context where the changes generally have not been independent of the processes taking place outside the centre of world capitalism. Moreover, the new wave of technological change is, in part, rooted in the increased concentration and centralization of capital, and the consequent changes in production relations.

Since about the Second World War, progress in science and technology as well as in the related fields of transport and communications has accelerated and brought about radical changes in almost all elements of the production process. Examples include synthetic materials replacing raw materials, new energy sources like nuclear power, automation and the application of electronics to the means of production. The role of human labour has been significantly altered as science has become much more involved in the production process.

Progress in science and technology has affected the structure, scope and effectiveness of the whole system of mass communications and information. By providing new means for informing and manipulating public opinion, educating a mass public, influencing the culture of the general population (for better or worse) and providing various demonstration effects, it has contributed a lot to the shifts in inter-class relations, the position of traditional political parties and social organizations, the relationship between leaders and the masses, consumer habits, and social and political behaviour generally. It has strengthened both centripetal and centrifugal forces in international politics. There is an increased recognition by the public of interdependence and concern for world affairs. A certain world consciousness, at least in respect of the dangers of a nuclear holocaust or an ecological catastrophe, has emerged.

Scholars disagree on whether one or more than one revolution in technology has taken place since the Second World War. They are also divided on whether human society has been blessed or cursed by this progress.

As already mentioned, it seems reasonable to distinguish at least two waves in the post-war development of science and technology. The first post-war revolution in science and technology was marked by automation, computer technology, the production of synthetics, nuclear energy and space research. The second revolves around the most recent results of electronics such as the miniaturization of microprocessors, computer-assisted design and computer-aided manufacturing, multi-purpose industrial robots, biochemistry, informatics, biotechnology (genetic engineering and manipulation), space technology, energetics and the production of even more new synthetic materials. This latter wave of technological advance does not merely represent a follow-on from the former revolution. It is a more intensive and complex phase in the development of science and technology. And it owes its causes to changes in world economic conditions since the early 1970s which have induced a considerable shift in factor proportions and resource requirements in favour of energy- and raw material-saving and environment-protecting techniques.

A certain alteration has taken place also in the general appraisal of the social, political, cultural and ecological effects of the scientific and technological revolution. The former euphoria and exaggerated hopes about its benefits which had been widespread in intellectual circles in the industrialized countries, have been increasingly replaced by criticism and scepticism since the early 1970s. On the other hand, the naïve illusions of its former opponents among some radical leftist and Third World scholars about the virtues of local traditional technologies and technological self-reliance for underdeveloped countries have also been increasingly supplanted by a more realistic approach.

As is well-known, the scientific and technological revolution initially originated in the military demands of the Second World War. With the end of the war, the military-oriented new technologies and scientific results spread into the civilian economy, but rather unevenly both across and within the countries concerned. Very soon, new and increasing military demands arose with the start of the Cold War and its renewed arms race. Once again this gave an impetus, and also a biased direction, to scientific research and technological development, particularly in those countries in the forefront of rearmament.

It was the US economy which gained the most advantages from the first wave of the scientific and technological revolution. Several factors worked in its favour. There were the vast sums of money required for research. The war had damaged the European industrial countries in their physical plant and human capital. Many qualified scholars emigrated to the United States. The overall result was that the post-war economic hegemony of the United States was greatly strengthened, as was its role in shaping the post-war international economic order, and the new trade and monetary institutions and agreements.

It was only after a period of reconstruction and by means of regional integration that Western Europe could hope again to overcome its technological lag behind the US. As for the USSR, it only managed to catch up with the US in military technology related to its defence requirements, and then only partially so and at the price of enormous efforts. Moreover, a technological development gap opened up between the military and civilian sectors of the Soviet economy. Japan, thanks to her enforced demilitarization, concentrated on the technological development of her civilian economy and succeeded eventually in gaining a leading position in several sectors.

The non-industrialized countries, including a majority of the developing countries, had to suffer a further widening of the international development gap.

The invention of strategic weapons of mass destruction has slowed down economic development and drained off economic resources. It has also led to a situation for the first time in history where the actual use of the accumulated stock of nuclear weapons in a possible unlimited war would cause the extinction of humankind.

The scientific and technological revolution may only have advanced, and even then very unequally, in the developed industrial countries of the centre and further widened the international development gap, but it has exercised a decisive impact on the world economy. Its effects on restructuring the world economy and world market have proved very substantial.

It has caused considerable shifts in the production and consumption patterns of the developed economies. It has created dynamic new industries. It has also led to the development of whole new generations of products. It has modified both input and output structures and, consequently, the pattern of international trade. One particular consequence has been its impact on the demand for commodities supplied by the underdeveloped periphery.

There has been a general shift in demand in favour of more sophisticated, research- and technology-intensive industrial products produced by highly skilled labour. And in particular since the energy crisis and awareness of the ecological danger, there has been a demand for energy-saving and environment-protecting technologies.

The first wave of the scientific and industrial revolution exerted its most conspicuous impact on demand for traditional raw materials as a result of the expanded production and utilization of synthetic materials. The substitution of these materials for traditional ones caused a serious deterioration in the world market position of a number of developing countries whose exports of primary products were adversely affected. At the same time it temporarily reinforced the upward trend in demand for crude oil, both as an energy source and as a raw material for the production of synthetics. This contributed to a greater differentiation among the developing countries.

The scientific and technological revolution, contrary to the naïve illusions appearing in the economic literature of the 1960s, did not prove capable of solving the natural resource problems of the world. It was unable to reduce the need for *all* primary products. This was inevitable, given the inputs required by the production of synthetics, which necessarily involve natural raw materials, including energy supplies. Another reason was the social conditions under which this revolution unfolded, namely the demands, manipulated by business interests, of Western consumer society. This not only squandered the cheap raw materials supplied by the developing countries in competition with each other, but almost institutionalized the practice of accelerated obsolescence, deliberate reductions in quality, and rapidly changing waves of fashion.

The shift in the consumption patterns of the highly developed capitalist countries is of course not only connected with the scientific and technological revolution. It also comes about as a result of the general increase in real incomes. This, in turn, has emerged due to domestic economic growth and welfare measures, partly made possible by increased international exploitation. The overall outcome has been a shift in consumer demand towards commodities of a higher order, i.e. durable consumer goods.

However, owing to the distorted operation of this consumer society, with its business-manipulated fashion changes, brand wars and advertisement-induced status symbols, this shift has assumed exaggerated proportions. It is increasing to the detriment of other sectors of need, such as cultural and educational development.

By increasing the concentration and centralization of capital primarily in the new industries and by accelerating the internationalization of capital, the scientific and technological revolution has stimulated the rise of a novel type of capitalist company: the multinational or transnational corporation which controls several, often unconnected, industrial branches at a time.

The effect of the scientific and technological revolution has manifested itself also in the massive growth of the material forces of production. Their requirements in terms of investment and marketing have expanded hugely, both horizontally and vertically. The growth has also played a decisive role in the contradictory acceleration of the concentration and centralization of capital, contradictory in the sense of producing a new role for decentralized capitals, too. It has facilitated state intervention which has become more and more necessary despite the rise of new non-state mechanisms of regulation, because there have to be institutions to handle integration tendencies and regulate changes in economic relations between the developed capitalist countries.

The first wave of the scientific and technological revolution made many of the traditional basic industries of the West rather outdated; some had to become 'run away' industries, others became heavily protected.

The new, second wave has brought about a radical shift in the technology mix in favour of, as we noted, energy- and raw material-saving technologies. Labour-saving technologies have spread rapidly into new areas, including administration, communications, commerce and the service sector. Due to its more complex nature, the higher speed of its unfolding and its wider and deeper penetrations into almost every sphere of society, the new wave of the scientific and technological revolution tends to be more important than the former in its impact on the development of societies and the redistribution of positions in the world economy. In particular, late-comers are much more heavily penalized than in the previous period.

The new wave has set up even more stringent requirements concerning the quality and discipline of labour. It similarly requires a more complex organization of the production process. Quality standards and technological parameters of inputs must also be higher. So must the qualities of management, planning, control and information. It has made international co-operation inevitable even for the biggest and most developed countries. Access to the latest research results and an ability to adjust flexibly and innovatively have become a decisive factor in international competition. The latter qualities have increasingly complemented or even replaced the advantages of economies of scale. A new role is now possible for some smaller but more versatile units in the economy.

The impact of science and technology, particularly its new wave, is now crossing national frontiers, and promoting the process of internationalization and globalization. The revolution in telecommunications, to take one example, easily renders even a country with a closed, autarkic economy subject to demonstration effects. And the most isolated and neutral countries are vulnerable to the new military technologies.

We do not yet know how far the new wave of STR will alter human society, how widely it will affect the relationship between nature and society, or the general social transformation of the world. The social sciences are lagging behind the natural sciences. But we can identify which are the negative or dangerous trends, such as the military bias in technological development and the widening development gap. And we do know what are the favourable, promising ones likely to advance human welfare, social security and cultural development, and to solve the problems of nutrition and resources, disease and pollution. And perhaps we also know enough to point out what fundamental changes are necessary in international economic and political relations if a more secure and egalitarian world order is to be developed, and also what internal changes in individual countries are required to overcome their subordinate position of underdevelopment.

Let us now look at the social relations of production in the capitalist centre of the world economy. Here a great change has been brought about by the coming into prominence of giant capitalist corporations. These vertically or horizontally integrated conglomerates reflect the increasing multinationalization of capital. Secondly, there has been the development of state monopoly capitalism in varying forms and intensity. And thirdly, the contradictory but accelerating process of regional economic integration as a concomitant of the establishment of supranational institutions. These changes, too, have had far-reaching consequences for the disruption and restructuring of colonial-type relations and division of labour.

The Transnational Corporations

The contradictory nature of the transnational corporations is reflected in the heated international debates on their role and impact.[76] Their dual nature follows from the objective contradiction between their role in promoting the inevitable tendency towards the internationalization of productive forces on the one hand, and their simultaneous role in expanding capitalist socio-economic relations involving inequality, domination and exploitation, on the other. No realistic alternative or counter-strategy can be found unless this contradictory nature of theirs is duly considered. Instead of romantic nostalgia for some outdated form of capitalist enterprise or for closed national economies, a carefully co-ordinated set of actions against their harmful effects is required, i.e. what is needed are preventive measures to avoid the dangers posed by them and a search for ways of transforming them and alternative forms of internationalization and co-operation.

Changes in the pattern of capital flows and investments reflect, in addition to structural changes in production and consumption, certain new motivations and interests on the part of the giant firms. The TNCs endeavour to ensure, along with an increased flexibility in adjusting to rapidly changing market conditions, technological complexity and institutional insecurity by building vertical links of production into their corporate system. This motive stems from the increasing necessity for close relations between the vertical links in production. This is because of greater precision in the specification of products, component parts and basic materials, the ever more complex technological inter-relations and the requirement that inputs should be available at the right time, in the right quantities and of a standard quality. Closer vertical integration also follows from the inadequacy of an anarchic market mechanism to cope with such technological relationships. The TNCs are trying to resolve within the company system the contradictions originating from the anarchy of market spontaneity. This makes it necessary for them to include their co-operating partners in their corporate system, i.e. to acquire effective control over them.

So the transnational corporations have expanded their activities and increased their penetration of fields formerly monopolized by metropolitan national capital. The business interests of different national capitals have become more and more intertwined in their corporate system. And the whole process of multinationalization of economic relations has forged ahead. All this has contributed to the crisis of the colonial pattern of the international division of labour. The primarily bilateral relations of the latter system — between the metropolitan centre and the individual economies of its periphery which originated within the system of empires — have increasingly broken up. Instead they have been replaced by multilateral relations since the collapse of the colonial system and the progressive internationalization of capital.

Many of the TNCs have been pioneers in the transition from a colonial to a neo-colonial policy. The TNCs' capital export and investment policies have been perhaps the most decisive 'internal' force which has brought about changes in the capitalist division of labour between the centre and the periphery. To take but one example, the spectacular growth in industrial output and exports of the newly industrialized countries is mostly connected with the role of TNCs.

The post-war hegemony of the United States has been another factor bearing upon the disintegration of established bilateral centre–periphery relations within the bounds of former colonial empires. These relations had in any case become unstable as a result of the damage inflicted by the war on the metropolitan countries, as well as the advances made by liberation movements. And there was no possibility after 1945 that the United States might take over the colonial territories of the other metropolitan powers in the same way as Britain and France had done with the German colonies after the First World War. This time the forces of socialism and the strength of anti-colonial national liberation movements precluded such a possibility.

Moreover the national economy of the United States was rich in natural resources and possessed the most developed agriculture in the world. The maintenance of a colonial type of international division of labour appeared to be much less necessary for it than for the earlier leading metropolitan powers.

In addition, the period of reconstruction after the Second World War involved essential structural changes in the countries of the centre which compelled the periphery countries to adjust and accept a modification in the colonial specialization system itself. In the process of such an adjustment, the local conditions of periphery countries varied widely and presented different advantages or disadvantages, which explains the geographical shifts in the 'development of underdevelopment' between different periphery countries.

The rise of numerous newly independent states in the former colonies also challenged the pattern of centre–periphery relations in the capitalist world economy. Though the advanced capitalist countries, under US leadership, managed to establish a modified international economic order with the Bretton Woods Agreement and so on, and this did herald the more or less smooth operation of the centre at least, the above challenges have marked new potential counter-forces in the world economy.

State Monopoly Capitalism

The post-war period has also witnessed, as already mentioned, a transition to a system of state monopoly capitalism in the advanced industrial countries. This involved the introduction of the policy of state intervention to counteract downturns in the business cycle, and also welfare measures.

The rise of state monopoly capitalism in the 1930s (often in fascist guise initially) and the post-war extension of its Keynesian welfare state variant have been the responses of the system in the centre to those accumulation crises and dangerous socio-political tensions which appeared in the dialectical process of internationalization and monopolization, as a result of substantial shifts in internal (class) and external (inter-state) power relations. Just as the transition from *laissez faire* competitive capitalism to monopoly capitalism, with its 'organized capitalism of cartels and trusts',[77] had by no means eliminated competition, but had merely given the latter new, monopolistic forms and methods, so this transition to state monopoly capitalism has by no means eliminated 'the fragmentation of the control of capital'.[78]

State monopoly capitalism, we must be clear, is not a state with monopolistic power over the capitalist process of reproduction and accumulation, or a total centralization of capital. It is merely a new, modified relationship between the power of capital and the power of the state, with new functions being assigned to the latter. These new functions include damping down class struggle by means of corporatist 'social contracts', 'new deals', and so on. Trade union bureaucracies and social democratic leaders now tend to be associated with the machinery of power. Another variant is to militarize the whole society and mobilize its frustrated forces by chauvinist and racist calls to arms against an external or internal enemy. Other techniques involve intervening in the economic process by Keynesian demand-generating policies and welfare measures. Or monetarist policies favouring big business and supporting it by increased military expenditures may be used. The state may promote research and development for the expansion of exports or for military projects, etc.

From the point of view of whose interests are served, it makes of course quite a difference which of the above variants are chosen. State monopoly capitalism may imply the power of a military–industrial complex or it may institute a social democratic welfare state. It may either polarize the propertied and the immiserated classes or result in a more equitable distribution of income.[79]

Not even the most progressive application of Keynesian policies under social democratic leadership, however, has ever affected substantially the basic ownership relations of society. Nor have its promises of democracy implied real popular participation in the control of the national economy's capital accumulation process. Nevertheless the Keynesian variant of state monopoly capitalism has increased the role of the state in the economy. And it has given the opportunity to other social forces as well to influence the operation of monopoly capital and benefit therefrom. It has been fashionable in recent years to criticize Keynesianism and attribute its failure to state intervention in the economy for social welfare purposes. It has been blamed for the high costs of labour and the expense of social policies. But the crisis of Keynesianism has really been due to the fact that its regulatory mechanisms have been confined to *national* economies, while the increasingly transnationalized processes of capital accumulation and relocation of production have remained largely unregulated.

The recent wave of monetarist counter-revolution, with its neo-liberal rhetoric and neo-conservative practice, has been in fact induced by the need for a state-monopolist attempt to cope with the global crisis. Countries like the US and Britain have sought to limit the decline in their position in the world economy. They have done this at the expense of once again widening the social gap at home and shifting the burdens of recovery on to partners abroad. This experience leaves, however, the state monopoly nature of contemporary capitalism in the centre largely unaltered. The direct linkage between the state and the economy has continued. Under monetarism and Reaganomics, this was manifested in the reoriented distribution and fiscal policies of the state in favour of the rich and the promotion of big business by state-induced demand for armaments. The result has been the growing indebtedness (and dependence) of the state *vis-à-vis* finance capital. Monetarism has also undermined the former 'social contracts for class peace' within society and sharpened the inequalities and imbalances in the world economy. Even rivalry within the centre has increased and nationalist reactions among partners grown. This threatens to turn the zero-sum game of international trade into a negative-sum game for the world economy as a whole.[80]

All that has been said about state monopoly capitalism shows, besides its other general and more or less permanent features, its two-faced nature. This reflects its double task related both to regulating domestic social conflicts and ordering global economic competition under the new conditions that have prevailed since the Second World War.

Another important feature of this stage in world economic development which we must not neglect is the process of regional integration. In Western Europe a common market type of integration developed, originally only between the more or less highly industrialized countries. The way had been prepared for this by the process of micro-integration, i.e. co-operation and mergers between firms as well as international factor mobility. It was prompted, besides the political considerations *vis-à-vis* the socialist states of Eastern Europe, mainly by the aim to catch up with the bigger and technologically more advanced economy of the USA. It was hoped to provide private capital with better conditions, a wider market, expanded resource facilities and economies of scale.

In Eastern Europe the regional integration process started partly as a defensive reaction to Western trade policy and partly as a means to accelerate the development of productive forces, particularly in the less developed countries. It was hoped that the necessary structural transformation and establishment of basic industries would be helped by mutual supplies and technological co-operation agreed upon by the states concerned. Comecon has developed only rather slowly and almost exclusively as a form of macro-integration. There is still very limited inter-firm co-operation and joint enterprises on the micro level. The goal is an organized regional division of labour and planning co-ordination system across states. The current relinking of the Eastern European economies with the world economy and the necessary move to an intensive stage of development in these countries have put the introduction of new forms of co-operation, including micro-integration, on the Comecon agenda.

In the Third World regional integration has also progressed in one way or another. It has usually been of the common market type but has also made use of some planning co-ordination techniques. It has been motivated by the aim to defend common interests, to increase their joint bargaining power position versus external economic powers (as in the case of the Andean Pact), and to accelerate economic development and structural changes. Sometimes the purpose is the more limited one of maintaining certain common institutions, including infrastructure and market facilities, inherited from the past and utilized by national capital or transnational companies.

The most typical feature of the current stage of capitalist development has been the strong diversification of military, political and economic relations. While the world economy had remained under the dominant influence of the centre of world capitalism and its monopoly capitalist powers, the increase in number and defensive power of socialist states, and in particular the growth of Soviet military strength, has made for an international military balance of power. This kind of bipolarity involves both advantages and disadvantages. At the same time the diversification of international political and diplomatic relations has gone even further than what one might expect purely from changes in economic power relations. This is partly because of the entrance of so many new states into the international community. At the UN, the developing countries now have a voting majority, and Third World political power is now a significant factor in international diplomacy.

In addition, Third World countries vary more and more in terms of the world market position of individual countries or regions, the choice of socio-political development paths, and the rise of some new socialist regimes. This increasing differentiation in the Third World has made the pattern of international relations even more complex and controversial than ever before. And it points to the increasing complexity of the transformation process of the world and the ways in which events in one part can have an influence on the other parts.

The Rise of a New Pattern in the International Division of Labour

As has been already stressed, after the Second World War and the disintegration of the colonial system, the pattern of international capital flows and direct investments changed considerably. This was as a result of the scientific and technological revolution's impact on production and consumption structures and business interests, as well as the rapid growth of TNCs and shifts in international power relations. A large-scale redeployment process has now started. And it is tending to alter the structure of international specialization and the allocation of roles in the global division of labour. It has manifested itself in the rapid rise of certain industrial activities in some periphery and semi-periphery countries, so called run-away industries, and in the rise of newly industrializing countries themselves. The overall pattern of foreign investments in the Third World has altered.[81] And, more recently, there have also been changes in the relationship of the socialist economies with the world economy.

As a result of the considerable shifts in the production and consumption patterns of the advanced capitalist countries and the massive substitution of synthetic materials for natural ones, the colonial type of international division of labour — namely between the industrial centre and the primary producing periphery — has been increasingly undermined. In addition, the political changes in the Third World, the collapse of empires and the rise of a great number of new independent states with national ambitions, have also challenged the former international division of labour.

Increasing wage costs and problems of environmental pollution in the industrialized Western countries have prompted the transfer of some traditional labour-intensive and polluting industries to parts of the Third World. The marketing interests of those TNCs heavily engaged in the new industries strongly oriented to new technology have also led to a shift away from the colonial division of labour, in favour of a similarly unequal, but inter-industrial one. Parallel with the perpetuation of the colonial structure of production and export orientation of most of the developing countries and a further deterioration in their terms of trade after the mid-1950s, the outlines of a new division of labour have appeared. Its poles comprise the new leading industries based on advanced research and development which are more or less monopolized by the giant corporations in the West, and the technologically dependent, enclave industries producing or assembling consumer goods and intermediate goods in certain developing countries, mostly however still under foreign financial, technological and managerial control by companies of the centre.

The earlier investments of foreign capital in the periphery countries, i.e. those made in the colonial period and as a means of developing the colonial division of labour, had almost exclusively been concentrated in the primary producing, export sectors. Here cheap, unskilled labour from the traditional rural sector was employed. Labour-intensive technology was applied, and production, in compliance with the raw material demands of the metropolitan country, was, as a rule, export-oriented.

By contrast, new investment today prefers, along with some still important mineral sectors, to go primarily to those manufacturing branches which produce mainly luxury consumption goods or component parts. And they employ rather capital-intensive techniques even if these may be still relatively labour-intensive compared to plants in the metropolitan countries.

The industrial investments of the transnational corporations differ, of course, in the technologies applied, depending on the size of the domestic market which may suggest import-substitution industrialization or an export orientation. The skills of the available labour force are also relevant. The TNCs' choice of industrial investment fields seems to reflect one of three main models.

Three Models of Industrialization

The first model is import substitution. Here light industries use mostly capital-intensive imported technologies to produce a relatively luxury type of consumer goods for the high-income élite and expatriates.

This type of industrialization takes as its point of departure the inherited, distorted import structure reflecting extreme inequalities of income distribution. In principle, it is supposed to proceed backwards from the local manufacture of imported consumption goods to production eventually of intermediate and capital goods. In reality, it necessarily leads, as it did in many Latin American countries,[82] after a transitional period of easy import substitution, to a fiasco. The reason is the reluctance of foreign companies to develop local industry beyond a narrow range of consumer goods. They do not wish to produce modern, research-intensive capital goods or establish local centres for research and development in Third World countries. As for consumer goods, the narrowness of the domestic market for these luxuries constrains any sustained industrialization on this basis.

The second model has grown out of attempts to find a way out of the failure of the import-substitution industrialization model. Another factor behind the second model of TNC industrialization in the Third World results from the centre of the world economy's drive to replace obsolete industries at home by new dynamic ones and to establish in a number of developing countries new industries producing intermediate and even capital goods primarily for export.

This change has been supported by a certain deindustrialization in the centre. Leading business circles and governments want to modernize the production structure and get rid of some outworn or crisis-stricken industries, for example textiles, tobacco, steel and some semi-processing branches. Many of the new industries established in the developing countries have been the result of the transfer of such industries and parts of the production process. These so-called run-away industries from the metropolitan economies are those which have become technologically obsolete, less competitive, less profitable due to their high wage costs, or increasingly uncomfortable because of the environmental pollution they cause.

This second-hand industrialization only affects limited parts of the Third World, and it does not make the economy of the countries concerned more integrated. It cannot therefore reduce the periphery's asymmetrical dependence on the centre of the world economy. Even if the proportion of foreign ownership in the economy does not grow, technological and market dependence on metropolitan corporations usually increases. This is particularly true in the case of those industries producing relatively luxurious consumer goods for export and also those which have been transferred to the periphery and are supplying their capital goods or intermediate products back to the metropolitan industries.

No doubt the transnational corporations involved in these export-oriented industries may provide marketing facilities abroad (mostly in their own enterprises) for processed and semi-finished export commodities. This partly explains why a number of Third World countries seek involvement in joint ventures with them, even at the cost of guaranteeing them massive infant industry state support, protection, subsidies, tax allowances, and depressed wages.

This kind of industrial development does shift the production structures of developing countries away from a merely primary product specialization. But many of these second-hand industries, even if not suffering unfavourable trends in world market prices, like steel and textiles, remain enclaves within the national economy, having very little or no linkages with the rest of it. This is particularly the case of those using imported inputs (except labour) to produce spare parts for export.

The third pattern of industrialization can be subjected to much the same criticism. It is also mostly initiated by the transnational corporations and results from the transfer to certain developing countries of certain modern branches of industry using imported high technology. Examples include industries producing or assembling personal computers, electronic gadgets, TV sets, video recorders, motor cars etc. It has particularly taken place in South East Asia, where the required industrial milieu — infrastructure and a disciplined, trained low-wage labour force — is available or can easily be created. The TNCs involved in this kind of industrialization can make enormous profits from the relative wage differentials between centre and periphery.[83] They also benefit from various allowances, privileges and other kinds of state support provided by the host countries, thereby improving their market competitiveness *vis-à-vis* the producers of the same products in developed countries.

No doubt, those newly industrializing developing countries hosting such industries and TNC activities also benefit and show a much better performance than others in terms of industrial exports and foreign currency earnings. The vigorous growth of urban industries and manufactured exports, however, does not always imply a lasting economic development. The actual pattern of industry and inter-sectoral linkages in the economy does not necessarily improve. The application of modern technology, though requiring trained labour, does not result automatically in the general development of an industrial culture or improvement in labour quality. Nor does it make a country technologically developed in terms of R and D.

Just like the other two patterns of industrialization mentioned above, the refusal to transfer or establish in the newly industrializing countries research and development capacities for product and technology development remains a characteristic feature of the investment and management policy of the transnational corporations.

As for the social costs of co-operation with TNCs, these may prove to be very high in terms of the overall effect on the socio-economic structure, income distribution, social and cultural relations, as well as political conditions.

Nevertheless the possibility that the latter two models may lead to a breakthrough to a more wide-ranging and thorough industrialization process, with a concomitant development of an educated and skilled labour force, and even eventually progressive political changes, cannot be ruled out.

Consequences for the Third World

All the above three patterns of industrialization in the Third World point to the fact that a new type of international division of labour has evolved, at least sporadically, since the Second World War. This has grown up alongside the former, colonial type of international division of labour between the industrially developed centre and its primary producing underdeveloped periphery, which still exists and keeps many developing countries in a subordinate position.

The new division of labour still involves asymmetrical dependence and international exploitation, and may be called neo-colonial. It is still unequal and dualistic, but its two poles are less distinguishable in terms of *countries* because the new patterns of industrialization have affected the economic structure and social relations not just of certain developing countries, but also of the developed industrial nations of the centre. A number of traditional industries with their traditional working class have lost their former position there. Even if not closed down or transferred abroad, they have to face competition from the foreign subsidiaries of the TNCs and the cheaper products coming from the newly industrialized countries. As a consequence, unemployment has appeared again in several developed countries, and is not just of a cyclical nature. And the social contract with at least a part of the industrial working class has been broken or put in jeopardy.

The dichotomy involved in the new type of division of labour is nevertheless increasingly clear. On the one hand, there are the leading companies, mostly TNCs. These are based in the most developed industrial countries but have an international network of subsidiaries and clients in other countries. They represent the dominant, exploiting centre which tends to monopolize research and development capabilities and high technology. They control those industries, services, research and innovation activities which determine the development of modern technology and know-how. On the other hand, the periphery of the world economy embraces, besides the still primary producing developing countries, all those countries, including some of the former semi-developed as well as newly industrializing countries, which possess industry capable of applying, but not developing, the new high technology; they therefore remain heavily reliant and asymmetrically dependent on the imported technology developed by the centre.

The dangers and potential consequences of this division of labour follow from its inherent structural inequalities and also from the uncontrolled activities of the transnational corporations which constitute its driving force. Though an early adjustment to this new division of labour and co-operation with TNCs may provide advantages to the countries concerned, it depends on the *ways* of adjustment and co-operation whether the potential harmful consequences are realized or avoided.

Without regarding the TNCs as the devils of the contemporary world economy,[84] it should not be forgotten that they follow their own business interests and these hardly coincide with the host countries'. It is mostly in their own centres that they take decisions on their organizational, technological, investment and marketing policies. The horizontal international division of labour which materializes among the individual subsidiaries of these corporations through a vertical division of labour, may create a hierarchical system of decision-making. The top of that hierarchy is normally located in the centre of the vertical system, in the parent company.

The TNCs are making increasing use of new forms of investment, like joint ventures in which their equity does not exceed 50 per cent, and various international contractual arrangements not involving an equity capital contribution. These include management contracts, licensing and technical assistance contracts, franchising, turn-key and product-in-hand contracts, production sharing and risk-sharing contracts, international sub-contracting, leasing etc.[85] By playing an intermediary role in the increasingly inter-nationalized process of production in such key areas as the provision of technology, access to markets, or service areas like management, information, communications, training, and advice, the TNCs can extend and intensify their control over much wider fields than would follow from their actual investment activities and risk-taking.

The new ways in which foreign capital is deployed hardly lead to a decrease in the outflow of investment income from the developing countries, or to an appreciable improvement in their local capital formation. Transnational corporations have innumerable, usually hidden or indirect, possibilities to repatriate the returns on their investments, even under conditions of state supervision or where partial nationalization ensures the host country a majority of shares and positions in management.

The unfolding of this new division of labour and its concomitant changes in investment patterns reinforces the asymmetrical pattern of global inter-dependence and international exploitation. Through its structural impact it reproduces rather than eliminates the internal dualism of the periphery's socio-economic structures.

What follows is that not only the old, colonial pattern, but also the new emerging pattern, of the international division of labour exhibit glaring asymmetries, tendencies towards further inequalities, and other distorting effects on domestic structures in the periphery. As usual, both the harmful effects of the disruption in the colonial division of labour as well as the negative consequences of the current redeployment process have been suffered primarily by the less developed developing countries. This has been accompanied by an accelerated differentiation process within the Third World.

The deterioration of the Third World's terms of trade and cumulative indebtedness have proved to be rather general long-term trends characterizing the worsening position of most of the primary exporting developing countries in the world economy throughout this stage. This seems now to be the case even of the newly industrializing countries and major oil exporters. Recent trends in their balance of payments confirm this tendency, while indebtedness appears particularly characteristic of the major Latin American NICs.

The losses incurred by all developing countries from the deterioration in the terms of trade averaged about $5.3 billion in the first half of the 1980s. But this rose, due to adverse changes in the prices of non-oil primary commodities in 1980–83, to about $28 billion for 48 developing countries. Even the current account surplus of the majority of oil-exporting countries, which had resulted from the second price explosion in 1979–80, has turned into a deficit in recent years. In 1985 the real prices of non-oil commodities as a whole have fallen back to their lowest level since 1929–30, and real oil prices to the level they were at before the first price explosion in 1973.[86]

In 1986 the total external indebtedness of the developing countries reached 1,000 billion dollars. In 1985 the service payments they owed on this debt amounted to $131 billion.[87] In contrast, in the early 1960s, these figures in current values were only $24 billion and $4 billion a year, respectively.

Over the first five years of the 1980s, *per capita* gross domestic product declined in 59 out of 83 developing countries for which the relevant information was available. The total number of people living in poverty was estimated to be as many as 1.3 billion.[88]

It is clear that the process of redeployment and the structural changes in the world economy have not reduced, but rather sharpened, the global problems of underdevelopment, poverty and indebtedness in the Third World, even if some countries have managed to rise to a semi-periphery or relatively privileged position.

The latter, namely the newly industrializing countries, have responded positively to the above changes. By means of an open door policy, tax allowances, holding down wage levels and repressing trade union activities, they have created a favourable climate for foreign investment. They have been favoured as a result by the new capital export and investment policies of the TNCs. The result has been a spectacular growth in industrial output, exports, and the GDP generally. There has been a considerable shift in their economic structures as well as an inflow of some more advanced technology. Compared to the majority of developing countries still stuck in primary production and export, these NICs have gained a much better position in the world economy. But although industrial growth has taken place, this has not been accompanied by the establishment of an advanced national industrial base, with appropriate research and development capabilities. Production linkages across the whole national economy have not been set up. Instead, there simply exist industrial enclaves which cannot ensure benefits and better living conditions for the majority. All this development, in short, may turn out to be merely the reproduction of underdevelopment, albeit at a higher level. Some of the harmful effects of such a development have already provoked a theoretical critique.

The Socialist Countries of Eastern Europe

Turning finally to the socialist countries of Eastern Europe, as well as China, they missed out on the above changes in the international division of labour for a relatively long time. Only recently have their economies begun to be relinked with the world economy under the new conditions now prevailing. Before their socialist transformation, all these countries, except for the GDR and Czechoslovakia, had been unindustrialized or industrially underdeveloped countries, and belonged to the periphery or semi-periphery of the capitalist world economy. Thus in the first stage of their socialist development, their development strategies necessarily involved, besides fundamental changes in ownership relations and other dimensions of socialist transformation, the historically inherited national task of overcoming underdevelopment. The task was to establish an internally integrated, industrialized, self-reliant national economy, no longer specializing in primary production. There was no alternative if the political independence of these countries and the survival of their new regimes were to be secured. Nor could the introduction of the scientific and technical revolution in these countries otherwise be possible. The implementation of these goals has been started, though not yet completed everywhere and in all respects. But they have been achieved under conditions of international isolation not of their own making. What they had to endure was a politically motivated and enforced delinking from the capitalist parts of the world.

The East European model and strategy of development which emerged in the 1950s have been shaped by at least three equally important factors. Firstly, the local, historical specificity of their position, namely the relative backwardness of these countries, each with its own historical traditions and modernization tasks. Secondly, the international conditions of the time, namely their isolation during the Cold War and confrontation with the Western powers (it was this politically and ideologically hostile environment which gave birth to the bloc and underlined its military aspects and security considerations). And thirdly, the specific tasks and real or assumed laws of socialist transformation.

The above factors, of course, cross-cut each other, with the result that the national and class content of each country's actual development strategy got mixed up — the one sometimes reinforcing, and sometimes contradicting, the other.

One of the main features of the early model of Eastern European socialist development[89] was its stress on the extensive type of development. This assumed abundant and perpetually available natural resources and labour resources. It was also based upon heavily centralized accumulation and investment of surplus, which was mostly siphoned off from agriculture or gained at the expense of low consumption.

Another feature, implicit in the above, was the priority given to quantitative growth of the economy. Coupled with this was the concept of catching up with the advanced capitalist countries in the development of productive forces.

An accelerated, large-scale, non-selective and basically import substitution type of industrialization with a strong bias towards heavy industry was the result. The model revolved around more or less autarkic economic policies with only a limited role for foreign trade which in any case was directed mainly towards the other countries belonging to the alliance.

This pattern of accelerated industrialization imposed heavy burdens on agriculture because of its system of compulsory deliveries, taxation and other surplus-appropriating methods. It also, as mentioned, kept personal income levels under pressure by neglecting consumer goods production. The aims were to overcome historical underdevelopment, catch up with the Western industrial countries as soon as possible, and provide for an effective defence under the conditions of the Cold War.

The closing off of the Eastern European economies and societies from the West was primarily the consequence of the Cold War with its trade embargoes and political hostility from the West. Strangely enough, it was not the result of some considered policy on the part of Eastern European governments themselves to delink temporarily from the dominant centre of the world economy, and thereby eliminate economic dependence and exclude those negative demonstration effects of Western consumerism which would create obstacles to a basic needs oriented industrialization.

A further characteristic of the first stage of socialist development in Eastern Europe was the excessive role and massive intervention of the state in the economy.[90] This involved an over-centralized system of economic management and national planning with detailed instructions emanating from the capital.

A very important and to some extent synthesizing feature of the early East European model of development was the centralized system of decision-making in practically all spheres of social life under the control of the hegemonic party. Despite the principle of democratic centralism, this hardly left any room for mass participation in either the preparation or implementation of decisions.

This early model or strategy of development brought about many positive results, but also a host of unfavourable phenomena and consequences. The latter have become increasingly obvious as the process of transformation and development has progressed, particularly in the light of changes in the capitalist world economy.

Isolation from the West was always an abnormal and undesirable phenomenon. But undoubtedly it did contribute for a while, at least in the beginning, to the realization of a high rate of accumulation and economic growth by keeping away the negative demonstration effects of Western consumer society. It also prevented a mass brain drain and in this way contributed to the qualitative improvement of the labour force. On the other hand, it kept out the positive demonstration effects, too, and prevented the required flows of information and international co-operation in science and technology, thereby causing unnecessary duplication and high costs in R and D activities.

The autarkic policies of the 1950s resulted in serious losses, particularly for the smaller countries. It led to the establishment of uneconomic industries and caused structural imbalances and distortions. Despite Comecon co-operation, the industrial structure which evolved in each country under the conditions of individual and regional autarky, came into conflict with the new world market conditions. Eastern European countries' industrial structures were out of line with the new production and consumption patterns in the world economy, particularly in the Western economies. And they were isolated from, and could not cater to, the requirements of the new wave of the scientific and technological revolution.

These industrial structures, except for a few dynamic branches, mostly corresponded to those of industrial countries prior to the new technology. In fact, they reflected the false concept of having to go through all the same stages of industrialization as the West. Sooner or later, an industrial restructuring had to come on the agenda. This was particularly necessary for the smaller Comecon countries which can realize comparative advantages only in a few (if any) narrow fields of international specialization. They certainly cannot afford to develop simultaneously all the main industries. Such a restructuring became necessary also for other reasons: the further development of regional integration within Comecon and increase in consumer demand. The latter made imperative the development of formerly neglected consumer goods and service industries.

In addition to the above factors prompting change, the continuation of an extensive type of economic and industrial development became less and less feasible as the necessary resources, particularly labour reserves, became exhausted.

The rapid development, extensive industrialization and internal integration of Eastern Europe's national economies made them become more and more complex. A contradiction developed between the ever widening variety of goods being produced and the manifold interlinkages in the economy, and the more or less unchanged machinery of central planning and management. This contradiction spawned an ever growing bureaucracy, which was not a solution. Thus changes in the economic planning and management system became sooner or later inevitable in these countries. In addition, the growing diversity of consumer demands to be satisfied and the need for effective economic incentives also called for greater room for the market and monetary relations.

Despite the obvious achievements in establishing many industries based on advanced technology, the socialist countries of Eastern Europe have not yet achieved the full advantages even of standard modern technology, let alone the latest wave of high tech. If they do not make substantial changes in development strategy, they face the danger of a widening technological gap with the West again. It has to be conceded that, up to now, the technological development of the Eastern European economies has been uneven and not very efficient.

In the late 1960s and early 1970s, East–West relations began to normalize somewhat and Eastern Europe began to develop economic co-operation with the Third World. This partial relinking of the socialist economies with the world economy started at a time when world market conditions were still relatively favourable. The Eastern European socialist states hoped that they would now succeed, without too much difficulty, in realizing a rapid transition to the stage of intensive development. This was to involve the essential restructuring and technological modernization of industrial production parallel with an increase in living standards. It was necessary to satisfy the consumer demands which had exploded under the impact exerted by developing East–West trade, tourism and communications. These goals and hopes were based on the assumption that the détente process which had started in the mid-1960s would lead to a radical reduction in military budgets, thereby releasing considerable resources for economic development. They also assumed the elimination of all Western discrimination in trade and finance and the opening up of Western commodity and capital markets to Eastern Europe. The prospects for this seemed to be reinforced by the fact that the growth rate of the Eastern European economies remained high (far exceeding the world average).

But in the mid-1970s, the Western economies went into recession. The result was a contraction of markets, serious disturbances in the global monetary and financial system, and protectionist measures against imports. Moreover, the on-going arms race kept the military burden on Eastern Europe at a high level. The results were serious.

Imports of Western technology and consumer goods needed for modernization and by the mass of consumers respectively, were increasingly financed by foreign loans. The terms of these loans then deteriorated, exports did not grow dramatically, and the escalating debt-servicing burden caused several socialist countries growing difficulties.

It remained true, however, that the exhaustion of natural resources and increasing local costs of production combined with the region's relinking with the world economy, increased participation in the world division of labour and the sharpened competition in the world market to make a transition to an intensive type of development inevitable. This meant greater work intensity and labour discipline, but also higher productivity and research intensity. These factors had to become the primary engine of development rather than expanding the numbers of the work force. Otherwise Eastern Europe would face the risk of falling back to a periphery position in the world economy and losing those advantages of its former rapid growth which had helped consolidate and legitimize its new socio-economic system.

The East European socialist countries have succeeded in eliminating most of the basic causes and traditional features of underdevelopment. They have almost caught up with or are approaching the industrially developed West in several fields of economic and technological development. But now they have to face the new challenge of a transforming world economy. They have to respond to its new wave of technological advance and redeployment processes if they are to avoid a worsening in their world economic position.

5. A Structural Crisis in the World Economy

Crisis?

As already stressed, the colonial pattern of the international division of labour between the primary producing underdeveloped countries and the advanced industrial metropolitan countries has been facing growing difficulties. This is as a consequence of its built-in imbalance and the changes in technologies, industrial structures and consumption and investment policies since almost the Second World War, and particularly since the mid-1950s. The crisis of this inherited division of labour has become especially apparent in the light of the economic and political developments of the 1970s, primarily the so-called energy crisis and the successful economic pressures put on the West by the oil-producing group of developing countries.

The decreasing world market prices of primary products in the second half of the 1950s, the general deterioration of the terms of trade for the developing countries from then right through to the early 1970s and the increasingly cumulative process of these countries' indebtedness have been warning signs that this unequal division of labour with its lopsided specialization of the developing countries could not be maintained for ever. The fact that the world market position of the majority of developing countries has been further deteriorating since then and that their employment and nutrition problems have become worse, provides further evidence that the old structure is untenable.

These and other factors characteristic of the fourth stage of capitalist development explain why the world economy had to enter a phase of deep and lasting crisis again in the 1970s, after a relatively long period of stability.

All those inherent contradictions of the capitalist world economy which had been surfacing from time to time and managed separately before, have come together since the early 1970s. The key contradiction here has been the acceleration of the transnationalization of the reproduction process, and consequent internationalization of productive forces, conflicting with the unequally structured social relations of this internationalized production and the world's nation state-centred institutional system. Also of decisive importance has been the disintegration of the framework of empires which had previously kept the contradictions and disequilibria between centre and periphery as economic sectors producing for each other localized. And finally, there is the equally crucial historical factor of the relative normalization of East–West relations and the growth of economic relations between the socialist countries and the Third World. The former factor has brought centre–periphery conflicts to the forefront of inter-state relations. The latter has made the conflict of two different systems, which had hitherto manifested itself only as an international political, military and ideological confrontation between two, economically more or less isolated blocs, now an organic element of the world economy. The interactions of these two different but historically linked conflicts within a single world economy mark (besides the effects of the new technological revolution) the new era in world economic relations.

It is, of course, debatable whether the term crisis correctly expresses this change and whether, if such a crisis exists, it is cyclical or not. No doubt, the world economy as a whole will again enter a stage of relatively balanced recovery and expansion. But this is only possible once certain conditions are met. New institutions are needed for the global management of the increasingly global, transnationalized productive forces of the world economy. These institutions will have to be capable of reducing the unequal and asymmetrical social relations of production that currently characterize centre–periphery relations, and without recourse to continuous aid on the one hand and periodic external interventions and pressures on the other.

But whatever is the case — i e. whether the new era of the world economy is correctly called a crisis or not — it means, any way, a new challenge. The mounting disequilibria of the world economy are sharpening its immanent contradictions and speeding up its structural transformation. A battle is being fought not only for available markets but also for the redistribution of roles. Countries of the centre which used to have a dominant position before, can actually lose it. Those countries which began to catch up with the latter by adopting their structures are liable to fall back again to a periphery or semi-periphery position. In addition, it is no longer only national economies but different social systems which are competing with each other to adjust to the changing patterns of the single world economy.

In the eruption of the world economic crisis in the 1970s, a certain role was played (apart from some extraordinary events like the temporary oil embargo imposed by the oil-exporting countries or the decline in world food production caused by extremely unfavourable weather conditions in 1972) by the coinciding of certain cyclical changes in leading national economies. These cyclical effects combined with the fluctuations of an anarchic world market which was unable to regulate the increasingly internationalized productive forces, and also the internal disturbances of the monetary system.[91]

But beyond these factors there have also been more fundamental factors causing, perhaps for the first time, a structural and institutional crisis of the world economy as an organic whole. This is a crisis in the operation of the international division of labour and the global system for regulating the various national economies. This structural and institutional crisis can be traced back to various major factors, to which we must now turn.[92]

Causes

Shifts in International Power

Substantial changes have taken place, as already mentioned, in the international distribution of power owing to the development of socialist regimes, the collapse of the colonial system, the rise of anti-imperialist alliances and joint action on the part of the non-aligned countries, and shifts also in power relations between the developed capitalist countries. These changes have undermined the foundations of the earlier colonial type of international division of labour. They have even made it possible, in a given case and under temporarily favourable circumstances, to deal a blow against it. The oil embargo and series of oil price rises carried out by OPEC are the most obvious example where developing countries were able temporarily to change quite radically the terms of international economic co-operation imposed upon them by the monopoly/capitalist centre.

Owing to the collapse of the colonial system, the contradictions of uneven development and the economic imbalances inherent in the former bilateral relations between metropolitan countries and their colonies can no longer be so easily disguised or contained. They now manifest themselves in a whole variety of inter-state conflicts. The great number of newly independent states in the world, with their urgent demands and a voting majority in the UN General Assembly, has made it necessary to implement changes in the rules and machinery of both international politics and the global economy. The non-aligned movement put forward not only new political principles but also economic demands.

A sharpening contradiction has developed between the positive political changes that have occurred and the almost unaltered (colonial) pattern of economic relations between the developing countries and the metropolitan ones. This has led to both unilateral attempts and joint efforts to change the situation which in turn has induced neo-colonialist counter-reactions.

The economic demands of the non-aligned countries were reflected in the first UNCTAD international conference on trade and development, and those that followed. It led eventually to the demand for a New International Economic Order, as well as Third World producer associations and other devices aimed at changing the old terms.

The discrepancy between the political independence of the developing countries and their increasing economic dependence has shifted the focal point of the new stage in the Third World's struggle for national liberation to the field of economic relations.

Several developing countries have launched an attack on foreign capital occupying the commanding heights in their economies. They have carried through nationalizations, proclaimed a policy of self-reliance, and often also sought some degree of delinking from the developed industrial countries and the world economy which they dominate. In most cases the subsequent retaliatory measures, credit freezes, cessations of aid and trade bans have caused insurmountable difficulties leading often to military coups. In other cases the very weaknesses of these countries in terms of resources, skill shortages and inherited structural distortions of their economies have soon induced a shift in economic policy, once again providing wider scope for foreign capital and economic relations with the industrial centre.

The international system of economic institutions and rules of the game has also come under pressure. The Bretton Woods monetary system, the IMF, the World Bank and GATT, which were set up at the end of the Second World War, reflected the primary concerns and interests of the major actors and the economic power relations prevailing at the time. But they have come into conflict with recent shifts in power relations and the newly articulated interests of the developing countries. Long before the eruption of the 1970s crisis, this made it already necessary to revise some of the established rules. Let us explore these changes a little further.

The international system of trade, embodied in GATT, aimed primarily to generalize bilateral trade concessions by the application of the most favoured nation principle, and to reduce tariff barriers. It certainly met the acute need of the developed market economies to expand trade relations, first of all, among themselves and in the field of traditional commodity trade. But the GATT system completely ignored the interests of the structurally weak underdeveloped countries which badly needed non-reciprocal trade preferences. It ignored those countries with a socialist socio-economic system. And it failed to anticipate the rapidly growing trade in other fields such as the transfer of skills, technology and services, or the expansion of intra-firm trade across national boundaries taking place within the organizational framework of transnational corporations.

These new phenomena and omissions, as well as the increasing role of non-tariff barriers and restrictive trade practices and the rise of regional trading blocs (integrating whole regions) have all increasingly undermined the basic assumptions on which the GATT world trading system was built.

As for the post-war, Bretton Woods monetary system, this was predicated on a reserve currency exchange standard based on the US dollar. It assumed the dollar's convertibility into gold, and also fixed exchange rates. The whole system was actually based upon the dominant position of the US economy in the world. This was a viable assumption at first. After the Second World War, the dollar-hunger of the war-damaged economies of Western Europe and Japan reinforced the global supremacy of the US dollar. Later on, however, the US economy lost its post-war vitality.

There were many reasons for the decline of the dollar. The increasing outflow of US private capital for investment in the European Common Market (to strengthen its market position there), and also to the low-wage developing countries, was a factor. But more important was the paralysing effect of the rigidities introduced into the USA's industrial structure by militarization. The continuous priority given to weapons system technology diverted skilled personnel and R and D resources from the civilian sector. The run-away industries of US-based TNCs as well as the rapid catching up with them of their West European and Japanese rivals brought about a sharpening competition against US exports. The worsening trade position of the USA, along with its on-going foreign expenditures on military bases, overseas wars, mass tourism and aid weakened the US dollar, which was the very basis of the world monetary system, more and more. The eventual result was the abandonment of the convertibility of the dollar and of fixed exchange rates. This was partly a consequence of, and partly an aggravating factor in, the world economic crisis. It clearly revealed the contradiction of an international monetary system built on a single national currency.

Turning to the political changes since the Second World War, an increasingly obvious inconsistency has developed between global economic, political and military power relations. Economic forms of pressure, militarization and outright armed interventions have all influenced international economic relations.

The operation of the world economy has been affected by shifts in international power relations in another way. There have been changes in the geographical location of tensions and conflicts, in the structure of alliances, and in the means used to maintain or restore the balance of power. One consequence of this has been to increase inflationary tendencies in general, even before the oil price increases in the 1970s.

This trend in the West towards higher inflation has not just stemmed from government measures to counteract downward phases in the business cycle. More fundamental reasons for persistent inflation lie in the squandering nature of the consumer society, and the ever growing military expenditures induced by the arms race. This is one of the reasons for the appearance in the 1970s of the strange combination of accelerated inflation and stagnation. Though inflation has been successfully reduced recently by means of monetarist restrictions in the developed capitalist countries, this has been achieved, as a rule, partly at the expense of the social welfare budget (without touching on the major source of inflation, arms expenditures) and partly by pushing the cost on to other countries in the periphery where inflationary tendencies have by no means disappeared.

Redeployment

The redeployment process has involved the international restructuring of certain productive branches of the world economy, and a relocation of the structural roles of countries within it. This has also brought about substantial changes in the operation of the world economy. Not only have the mechanisms of the former colonial division of labour between the centre and the periphery been upset to the disadvantage of the latter, but the internal equilibrium of the economies of the centre has also been disturbed.

There has been increasing technological dependence both among the underdeveloped periphery countries and the socialist states, and even some countries of the centre which have been lagging technologically behind the most developed capitalist countries. Secondly, increased concentration of advanced technological research and development capabilities in the hands of the biggest monopolistic companies has taken place. These trends have strengthened the ground for monopolistic price formation in the case of many new technologies and advanced products, contributing thereby to inflationary tendencies in the world market. This is another factor, no less substantial and certainly more lasting than the oil price increase, which has tended to damage the terms of trade of all those countries badly needing to import both modern technology and crude oil. These countries were caught for a while in a pincer movement by both sets of price increases.

The redeployment process has led to the transfer of several outdated manufacturing industries from the developed industrial countries to the developing ones. Another outcome, where industries have not been relocated, has been their encountering an ever sharper competition from cheaper products from low-wage countries. In the absence of co-ordinated structural and social adjustment policies, the previous equilibrium based on the full employment achieved by post-war anti-cyclical policy has been destroyed. In some cases it has also undermined the position of certain strata of the traditional labour aristocracy in the West. As a consequence, the very basis of the welfare state has been affected both economically and socially. This points again to the fact that the crisis of the 1970s was prepared by processes which had started long before the oil price explosion.

Problems of Regulation

The increasing difficulties in using anti-cyclical, Keynesian policies of state intervention to regulate the operation of the national economies of the centre have been the result, primarily, of the sharpening contradiction between the national framework of their application and the actual ambit, much wider by far, of real economic processes. In other words, this crisis of regulation has an institutional character. It has appeared, because of the dialectical contradiction between national and international economic processes. While this tendency has accompanied capitalism throughout its history, it has become much more acute of late and has necessarily undermined the long-lasting effectiveness of anti-cyclical state intervention measures.[93]

The expanding activities and international networks of the transnational corporations have 'internationalized' an increasing part of international trade in the new form of transfers between their own subsidiaries operating in different countries. The consequence of this has been largely to exempt them from national control and normal market mechanisms. As a result, state interventions and anti-cyclical government policies have been rendered less effective.

This process has been accompanied by others such as regional integration, the progressive internationalization of productive forces, and a general increase in worldwide interdependency. This has tended to undermine the *national* economic framework which was the original target of all policies aimed at regulating economic processes.

Herein lies a paradox. The post-war period until the late 1960s saw the Keynesian recipe of anti-cyclical state intervention in national economies being widely introduced and more or less successfully applied in individual Western countries. But the same period also witnessed the growth of contrary tendencies which undermined the basis of these policies' success. This was the accelerated internationalization of production and capital, the worldwide sourcing and business activity of transnational corporations, the disruption of imperial systems which had kept the above contradiction of national regulation in an increasingly international economy latent, the multilateralization of economic relations in general, and progress towards regional integration. The fact was that the transnational corporations could easily escape from the effects of state intervention in a single country by using their subsidiaries and joint ventures to shift activity to another country. This fundamental fact points to the inadequacy of the national institutional framework for economic management.

Alongside, therefore, this increasing (and it should be noted, asymmetrical) interdependence between the various parts of the world economy, which has rendered the economic life of each country more sensitive to that of others,[94] an increasing anarchy in the world economy has come about in the wake of the spontaneous redeployment process carried out mainly by the TNCs, changes in the pattern of role allocation, and above all from the lack of an effective machinery of institutional intervention on the world level.

The increasing interdependence, and yet anarchy, of the world economy have made certain problems appear as global problems and captured public attention. Examples include the world ecological imbalance, environmental pollution, the exploitation of non-renewable natural resources, demographic and nutrition problems, etc. These global problems have appeared as symptoms or aspects of the world crisis, and have induced many economists to draw an apocalyptic picture of the future.[95] Though some of them may turn out to be less fateful than assumed, the continuing utilization of resources by the arms race and squandermania of the consumer society have been making these global problems worse and putting the brakes on economic development.

Consumerism
Thus a further factor has contributed to the eruption of the world economic crisis. This is the spread of a consumer society in the West since the Second World War, and its demonstration effects on other parts of the world. This consumerism has been frequently accompanied by deliberate reductions in the quality of mass produced goods, squandering, ostentation, and artificially created waves of fashion. It is based on the expanded credit system of the capital-rich Western economies as well as their cheap energy and raw material imports from developing countries. The demands of the consumer society have, therefore, not only exerted an increasing pressure on the world's non-renewable natural resources, but have also made it vulnerable to the vagaries of traditional sources of supply as well as to domestic credit conditions.

In addition, the demonstration effects of this consumer society have biased the consumption and import patterns of those countries which have imitated the Western example, and this has contributed to the worsening of economic imbalances.

Militarization

The crisis of the world economy has also been linked with global militarization and its effects. Even for those who simply attribute the eruption of the crisis to the oil embargo or to the accelerated inflation and instability of exchange rates (both symptoms rather than causes), it has to be clear that such phenomena all include certain military aspects. The very circumstances of the successful application of the oil embargo and price increases were closely related to military power relations. And in the acceleration of inflation, which actually started earlier than the oil price increases, and particularly in the rise of that strange symbiosis of inflation and stagnation (called stagflation), an important role has obviously been played by the armaments dynamic. This has slowed down economic growth while heavily burdening state budgets and forcing deficit financing which has contributed to both cost–push and demand–pull inflation.

Even if the present crisis were only the usual manifestation of a business cycle in the capitalist national economies, the role of militarization would be no less important. For heavy military spending may not necessarily boost anti-cyclical policies. It can actually be an obstacle if it reduces spending and the purchasing power of lower-income people. And to the extent that it increases transnationalization of the arms industry it runs counter to the existence of a national economy and limits the effectiveness of state intervention in it.

The international arms race and swollen military budgets all over the world, including the developing countries, have seriously undermined conditions for economic stability and development. By increasing unproductive expenditures and diverting investment funds away from human needs oriented production and services, militarization radiates out from countries where the profit motive and political goals originally induced it, and inevitably generates ever more severe inflationary pressures.

It follows from what has been said that the causes of the contemporary global crisis cannot be reduced to certain extraordinary or temporary events. Nor can they be derived merely from the normal business cycles of the developed market economies. This structural and institutional crisis of the world economy as an organic whole follows directly from the sectoral imbalances of the inherited system of the international division of labour, and the disturbances in its mechanism. These have been caused, as we saw, by shifts in international power relations, a redeployment process, disturbances of the national system of state regulation of the economy, the effects of a wasteful consumer society, and from the increasingly harmful consequences of the international arms race and militarization.

Consequences

In the past, economic crises affected individual countries or certain groups of countries rather than all of them. And if a crisis did become an international one, as in 1929–30, its epicentre could easily be identified and its effects traced.

But the present crisis has been affecting practically all countries, though in various ways and degrees.

The multi-dimensional nature of the present crisis is unprecedented. The interactions between the widely different processes and factors in world development have affected every conceivable aspect of economic life — energy supply, natural resource management, science and technology, the environment, population and nutrition, consumption patterns, life-styles, cultures, even political institutions and ideologies.

The contemporary crisis of the world economy occurs at a time when the very survival of humankind is threatened by the growth of the destructive capacities of modern armaments and millions of human beings are suffering from misery, hunger and sickness.

The most harmful effects of the global crisis have been on the majority of developing countries. Their world market position and internal economic conditions have worsened. The result has been that all those characteristics of crisis witnessed already since the late 1950s have become more acute, while the terms on which international assistance is rendered have also been toughened.

The annual rate of growth of all developing countries, which averaged about 5 to 6 per cent in the 1960s and in the first half of the 1970s, dropped to 1 or 2 per cent in the early 1980s. In the period 1980–84, growth averaged less than 1 per cent. *Per capita* gross domestic product in the periphery stagnated in 1980, decreased by 2 per cent in 1981 and decreased again by 2 per cent in 1982. In the period of 1980–84 as a whole, the growth rate of *per capita* GDP was 0 per cent or less in 70 developing countries, 0.1 to 1.9 per cent in 15 and above 2 per cent in only 21 developing countries.[96] In Latin America, for the first time since the Second World War, aggregate real income and investment declined and *per capita* income decreased by nearly 3 per cent in the early 1980s. The gravest consequences appeared, of course, in the very poorest countries, most of them in Sub-Saharan Africa, where agricultural output also decreased.

The process of growing indebtedness of developing countries has also speeded up. The total external debt of the developing countries reached nearly 1,000 billion dollars in 1986. The number of unemployed in these countries is estimated to be over 450 million.[97]

As for the developed market economies, despite some recovery, the crisis has proved to be a much more lasting phenomenon than expected. The traditional characteristics of recession have persisted — mass unemployment and underutilized capacity, weak investment propensities and sharpened competition. The average rate of unemployment in the OECD countries reached 5 per cent in 1974–75. It did not drop in the years that followed, but went up to 5.5 per cent in 1979, 6 per cent in 1980, over 8 per cent in 1981–82, nearly 9 per cent in 1983, and reached a record 11 per cent in 1985. The number of unemployed in the developed market economies now exceeds 30 million. There was a drop in, or very low rate of growth of, GNP in these countries throughout the 1970s and early 1980s. And the growth of productivity slowed down, marking the roots of the crisis in the capital accumulation process. The failure of even social democratic Western governments, the growing polarization within Western society, the erosion of the Welfare State and disillusion with Keynesian policies were symptoms of a deep-seated reality.

As for the Eastern European socialist countries, they were hardly affected by the world economic crisis until the mid 1970s. Since then, however, the various negative effects of the latter have affected them, particularly the increasing difficulties experienced in the necessary transition from an extensive to an intensive type of economic development in these countries. The results were unexpected imbalances, structural and technological bottlenecks, disturbances in the machinery for national planning and economic management, a slowing down of economic growth, worsening supply and balance of payments problems, and increasing indebtedness. Though the average rate of growth of the East European socialist countries remained higher than that of the Western capitalist countries throughout the 1970s, some of them (notably Poland) entered a deep economic and even socio-political crisis at the end of the decade. Those countries which were able to keep their economies in relative balance, or restore the equilibrium that had been disturbed by external effects, were only able to do so at the price of a radical slowing down of economic growth. In some cases, such as in Hungary, this became tantamount to stagnation. Real wage increases came to a halt or were even reversed. None of the socialist countries of Eastern Europe escaped a considerable decrease in growth rates, a trade deficit, increased foreign indebtedness, and a certain degree of inflation in the late 1970s and early 1980s. The annual rate of growth of the net material product of these countries, which had averaged 9 per cent in the late 1950s and more than 6 per cent in the 1960s and early 1970s, dropped to 4 per cent in the second half of the 1970s and decreased further to about 2 per cent only in the early 1980s. The share of personal consumption in the national income also decreased considerably because of increasing debt service payments.

However, these countries have managed to avoid such consequences and symptoms of crisis as mass unemployment. It is also to be noted that, since 1983, their economic situation has, in general, improved. The rate of growth increased again, and the most acute financial and debt-service problems were overcome in some of these countries.

Nevertheless the world economic crisis and its consequences have dispelled all illusions that socialist development could be an autonomous process independent of the world economy. No one thinks any more that there are unlimited possibilities to increase the efficiency of overall national planning and centralized economic management. A role has to be given to market forces. A completely new type of international economic relations and integration among socialist economies has to be built. And its pricing, accounting and monetary systems cannot be totally independent of world market conditions.

In conclusion, it is absolutely clear that we are indeed facing a one world crisis, a global institutional and structural crisis of the world economy, not three separate phenomena of crisis in three unconnected worlds, even though its roots and consequences are not equally distributed across the world map. This is so, whatever may be the responsibility of local factors in the deterioration of economic conditions and in disturbances of equilibrium. The business cycle with its regular recessions may be an inherent feature of the capitalist economies. But neither the deep economic crisis in the West, nor the development deadlock and further economic deterioration of the majority of developing countries, nor the new difficulties in the socialist countries' economies can be properly explained independently and separately from each other, i.e. outside the context of the world economy as a whole.

6. World Economic Transformation: Lessons and Prospects

Our knowledge of the general laws of operation of the world economy and the specific socio-economic, political, institutional and cultural conditions of individual countries may be incomplete. But our historical–empirical investigation of the development of the capitalist world economy and our theoretical analysis of the inherent contradictions and tendencies of the capitalist system do provide a sufficient basis for drawing conclusions as to the direction of the transformation that is needed, its motive forces and key issues.

Lessons from the Analysis of Capitalism and its World Economy

Capitalism as a social system has in general introduced economic coercion as the method for appropriating surplus. This has been substituted for the thousand year old methods of non-economic violence. Its history is the process by which monopolistic private ownership, which was originally established by non-economic force and which succeeded in excluding the majority of working people from property, eventually came to dominate the main means of production. The capitalist system was built on the appropriation of the surplus product of labour (the only creator of value) and its accumulation as capital. In this way, by means of its already appropriated and accumulated past labour, capital ensures and reproduces the conditions necessary for the appropriation of the surplus product of live labour. And so the cycle goes on.

This mechanism is the very basis of the antagonism between labour and capital, i.e. between live labour of the present and dead labour, appropriated in the past. It explains why the rules governing the allocation of social roles as well as income distribution are not identical for the two classes but rather dualistic: for the owners, it is basically capital ownership which determines social position, their role in the social division of labour, and their reward; while for the non-owners it is basically their own labour which determines these conditions, provided always they can sell it in the market under the conditions laid down by capital.

Individual freedom for the worker, free mobility and marketing of his or her labour, are the great achievements of capitalist society as compared to pre-capitalist ones. But economic coercion is the historical price of these achievements. Freedom for the worker only exists under conditions dominated by capital, including economically determined social inequalities.

Social Emancipation

What follows is that the transformation of the system into a post-capitalist society implies a process of social emancipation. This must involve the liberation of human live labour from the dominance of materialized dead labour (producer goods, in the parlance of non-Marxist economics), and the liquidation of the dualism in the rules determining role allocation and income distribution within society.

This process necessarily involves, usually indeed as its point of departure, the elimination of monopolistic private ownership of capital. It also, of course, requires a great many other changes in society, in its economic, political and cultural institutions. The replacement of private ownership of capital by public (state) ownership does not result in socialization *per se*; appropriate changes in the content, direction and control of the public sector are also essential. This means that a transition to socialism involves much more than some kind of association of the employed workers with the capitalist shareholders in the company. Nor does socialization of private ownership simply mean the participation of trade union representatives in the management of private firms.

The collective management of the economy requires socially controlled decision-making and the institutionalization of a socially owned economy. This requires new forms and effective machinery for political as well as economic democracy.

The replacement of dualistic rules by a single and universal set of rules governing the distribution of roles and income in society requires, over and beyond changes in ownership relations, guarantees of full employment and access to appropriate jobs in accordance with each person's knowledge and performance. All obstacles to social mobility must also be removed — not only those set up by capital ownership but also those stemming from educational or political monopolies. Free access to education and training, and opportunity to participate in political life, are therefore also a requirement.

But even the most developed institutional forms of democracy and the highest levels of social mobility possible cannot ensure real and massive participation in decision-making and control unless members of society are also intellectually interested in as well as morally prepared for such participation. Education must play a role in the development of collective consciousness and values.

It follows that such a transformation of society is not an over-night action but a long historical process. It will inevitably involve many experiments and mistakes, difficulties and diversions. Even the most general strategic issues mentioned above cannot be reduced to simple questions like the proportion of the economy in the state sector, the redistribution of the equity capital of private enterprises, the participation of workers' representatives in management, or the number of political parties, the degree of centralization or decentralization etc.

The process of social transformation also involves conflicts, and cannot be pushed forward without struggle by those whose social emancipation is on the agenda. This explains why the organized labour movement[98] is the basic social force of this transformation.[99]

The process of social emancipation cannot start directly on a world level. This is because of the primarily national framework of social life despite the internationally unequal pattern of social class formation. The nation state is the focus in the struggle of socio-political forces, and it is the nation state that guarantees the status quo, i.e. the existing order of social relations.

However, capitalism has developed not only as a particular system of society within individual countries, but also as a world system of economy with its dichotomy between a dominant centre of economically developed and well-founded national societies and a dependent periphery of economically underdeveloped, not yet strongly integrated societies. World transformation therefore necessarily implies also the process of national emancipation.

National Emancipation

Capitalism in a national setting, tied to the institutions and ideology of the nation state, inevitably results in a process of domestic class struggle. But, of course, it also involves the exploitation of other nations through the international activity of capital, and consequently, constitutes also an international arena of class struggle. The two aspects are therefore organically inter-related. In other words, the dialectical contradiction between the national and the international is the natural concomitant of the worldwide development of capitalism, and manifests itself in the whole variety of economic, social, political and other processes.

National emancipation, just like social emancipation, cannot be reduced to, let alone be achieved by, a mere declaration of formal equality, independence and political rights. In addition to a declared political sovereignty (which must be respected!) it must involve objective and subjective conditions, i.e. the basis of real sovereignty and equality, economic as well as cultural. Without overcoming underdevelopment, the developing nations cannot escape their economic subordination or cultural domination, and so become internationally emancipated.

Underdevelopment

The underdevelopment of developing countries can by no means be explained by the earlier social relations of traditional societies. Nor can any investigation not take into account the entire international system of capitalism. Underdevelopment does not represent simply a lagging behind. It is not some kind of earlier but natural phase of growth in the universal process of economic development, a situation which is sufficiently accounted for by its unfavourable internal relations. It is, instead, the product of a distorted and dependent development deriving basically, though not exclusively, from the development of the world capitalist system as a whole. The autonomous socio-economic development of these countries of the periphery has been interrupted and their further development blocked or distorted by the unfolding of the capitalist world economy. Their long-standing relations with the economies of the developed capitalist countries — as a result of commodity trade, including the slave trade, the flow of capital, financial and foreign exchange relations, labour migration and technological ties — have resulted in the formation of a system of asymmetric economic dependencies. This has led to a drain of income from them, based increasingly upon economic coercion (as a substitute for open, colonial non-economic violence), and the disintegration of their internal socio-economic structures as a result of foreign capital penetrating their economies, or market forces. Economic dependence, regular income losses and the distorted, disintegrated structure of the economy and society are the inter-related characteristics of underdevelopment which ensure its reproduction.

What may formerly have been endogenous legacies of the past — the underdevelopment of domestic market relations, the lack of technological skills, the low productivity of manpower, and the existence of traditional forms of consciousness and institutions — have become increasingly the consequence of a distorted internal structure caused by external forces and a distorted adjustment to world pressures. The population explosion, shortage of capital (i.e. limitations on internal accumulation), unemployment, and the low level of productivity are mostly the consequences of this distorted, disintegrated socio-economic structure, i.e. of the operation of peripheral capitalism itself.

In creating and maintaining this structure, a role was played not only by external forces but also internal ones. The latter adjusted to the requirements of the centre countries of international capitalism. Following their own narrow group or class interests, they chose not the national road to capitalist transformation but the blind alley of dependent, peripheral capitalism. The result was an extroverted economic development. This means the growth of export enclaves tied to the economies of the developed capitalist countries. It involves the unproductive squandering of incomes in a parasitic way, by imitating the luxury consumption of the countries of the centre. In the course of this, it has proved perfectly suitable to preserve pre-capitalist relations in certain parts of the economy and society, and even to apply pre-capitalist methods of exploitation. This is because the ruined but preserved pre-capitalist sector has become the source of cheap, unskilled labour and functions as the dependent supplier of semi-proletarian manpower, which constitutes merely a cost factor rather than a market for the capitalist sector.[100]

This dialectic of external and internal forces that has evolved basically as a result of the international expansion of capitalism, warns us not to neglect the external, international factors. Any other explanation of underdevelopment, for example in terms of inherent endowments, and choosing the national framework as the exclusive unit of analysis, leads inevitably to apologetics. It simply rationalizes and legitimizes the impact of world capitalism, and leads to the neglect of local class forces, interests and exploitation, including comprador responses and economic policies, within the periphery. It should be added, however, that blaming international economic relations for *all* implications of underdevelopment, or taking the world economy as the only appropriate unit of analysis, leads to no less apologetic conclusions protecting domestic reactionary and exploiting classes in Third World countries.

Thus the analysis, just as much as the search for a solution, has to extend simultaneously over international and national relations, and also over the developed and underdeveloped sectors of the world economy.

Dependence

No doubt, the most outstanding characteristic, as well as cause, of underdevelopment is external dependence. What is, however, often forgotten or not stressed enough, is that external dependence of an economy can take different forms, and the external dependence is also internalized — manifested in and connected with the internal structural deficiencies of the economy.

There are substantial differences between the various forms of economic dependence. The capitalist form of dependence *par excellence* is embodied in foreign ownership and control over the key sectors of the economy. Other more indirect forms include trade dependence, financial and monetary dependence, technological and educational dependence etc. These heterogeneous forms vary in respect of their duration, capacity to reproduce themselves, roots and manifestations, effects on production structures, and consequences in terms of income losses and international exploitation.

These forms may reinforce each other and culminate in an extremely intensive dependence of a country *vis-à-vis* some particular world power. This happens when the various lines of dependence converge. On the other hand, the opposite may occur and one form of dependency may partially counteract the effects of the others.

The very complex and changeable pattern of dependence may open up a relatively wide room for manoeuvre. There may be opportunities for dependent countries to diversify their partners or shift from one form of dependent relationship to another. In this way it may be possible to gain more independence even under overall conditions of dependence.

As regards the internalized character of external dependence, this manifests itself in the fact that the distorted and disintegrated socio-economic structures of periphery countries have been shaped by their adjustment to the centre of the capitalist world economy. It also involves a local centre–periphery relation between a dominant, extroverted (mostly foreign controlled) capitalist enclave sector and the partly destroyed, partly transformed and preserved, traditional sector. This dichotomy is the dualism we are familiar with. There are many consequences of this structure in respect of population growth, structural unemployment, obstacles to domestic market expansion and productive capital accumulation, social class formation, and so on.

What is called the development gap is the cumulative reproduction of the relative lag of the peripheral dependent economies behind the countries of the centre. It is the consequence of asymmetrical relations of dependence and unequal structures formed in the world economy. Behind these are hidden the international and internal (national) inequalities of social production relations.

These unequal relations of ownership and control stem from the international division of labour's allocation of roles, and determine the distribution of income.

Consequently, the bridging of this development gap, or liquidation of underdevelopment, cannot be achieved so long as these relations and structures remain unchanged. Merely altering the international distribution of income by increasing financial and technical assistance or improving the terms of trade is no solution.

Delinking

To escape from dependence and underdevelopment in the periphery, a policy of delinking and self-reliance has often been recommended. However, its actual feasibility depends on a range of factors — the scale and intensity of economic, political and other linkages with the outside world, and also on how cohesive are the social forces inside the country and the capability of the economy to sustain itself. Any neglect or miscalculation of such conditions may easily make the concept of self-reliance or delinking mere wishful thinking. The result may be failure — an electoral defeat, a *coup d'état* or a counter-revolution — for the political regime trying to implement such a policy.

It follows from the dialectics of the external and internal aspects of underdevelopment that, in considering a strategy of delinking, one must bear in mind the following:

⋆ Even if all contacts with the outside world are cut off, an underdeveloped periphery economy remains in fact extroverted and dependent because of its distorted structure;

⋆ As long as this internal structure prevails, it serves as a basis for new relations of dependence to arise;

⋆ A sudden politically or economically unprepared cutting of the economy from its dominant partners in the centre may cause, as several examples show and quite apart from any retaliatory actions by the latter, such serious dislocations in the economy's already established supply mechanisms that a crisis situation may develop which can easily be manipulated from outside and lead to a coup and the collapse of the regime;

⋆ A successful reduction of external economic dependence and a successful internal restructuring of the economy must go hand in hand.

In the light of the dialectical relationship between economic dependence and structural deformation and the complexities of peripheral capitalism's socio-economic relations, many debates about choices of development policy prove to be meaningless scholastic exercises. This goes for many of the debates on export-orientation or import-substitution; this type of comparative advantage or that; capital-intensive or labour-intensive technology; priority for industrialization or rural development; whether to co-operate with the TNCs or not, etc. The reason is that these economists take these issues, however valid in themselves, out of their multi-dimensional and dialectical global context.

The success or failure of a policy of delinking depends also on whether the world market is in a phase of expansion or contraction.

During a phase of world market contraction, particularly in time of war, delinking attempts are, as a rule, more frequent and intensive. This is because the normal ties of external dependence are, at least temporarily, reduced or broken. Also under such conditions, the limited gains (which only benefit a narrow élite) from the unequal international relations mostly disappear, and so society as a whole is more inclined to accept radical changes and undertake greater sacrifices in the hopes of a better future.

In a boom period of the world market, on the other hand, demand is growing and trade relations expanding. The opposite is then likely to be the case, and increasing resistance to a policy of delinking is likely to appear.

The success or failure of a policy of delinking is also affected by the ever increasing internationalization of productive forces in the world economy and the progressive transnationalization of science and technology. When any new technological or scientific revolution is unfolding, isolation from its birth-place can be particularly harmful. One must take into account also the wide differences between individual countries in respect of the actual level of their productive forces and their capacity to absorb and adapt new technologies. The nearer the level of a periphery country to that of the advanced countries and the greater its absorption/adaptation capacity, the more harmful the consequences of isolation are. That is not to say that countries with a lower level of technological development may not also be negatively affected by isolation.

Similarly, differences between countries in the size of their economies, available resources, and actual level of development of their productive forces will all affect the chances for a successful delinking policy. But the overriding determinant remains how far the world development of productive forces has reached.

What was possible in the past, or even relatively recently between the two world wars, is hardly possible now. Then at least a big country like the Soviet Union, rich in natural resources and under a new social system with centralized national planning, could restructure and develop its economy, despite its isolation, in the hope of catching up with the advanced countries in some key areas of development. But today the new stage of internationalization and accelerated process of scientific and technological revolution precludes this. For newcomers the distance required to catch up has grown immeasurably, as has the scale of contemporary productive forces to be absorbed. Indeed, in a national or even a regional periphery economy, conditions of isolation would today preclude the development of productive forces from ever reaching the contemporary world level. Not even the biggest and most developed countries of the centre can today afford to isolate themselves from the international development of science and technology without running the risk of lagging behind.

The capitalist world economy has developed into an increasingly organic unit. Worldwide linkages of the production process have widened and deepened the international division of labour. Capital has become ever more internationalized. So have science and technology. Nevertheless these developments cannot lead to the total absorption of national economic units by the world economy. The national framework of certain economic, social and political processes will not disappear. Even the process of the transnationalization of capital, as well as the transformation of local commodity production into world commodity production, come up against certain obstacles.

In fact, it is just because the development of the world economy has hindered the growth of integrated national economies in the periphery that a substantial number of these countries have made local efforts to end dependent, peripheral capitalism and create a real, integrated national economy. These efforts to gain relative economic independence counteract the globalization trends in the world capitalist system.

Thus capitalism as a world system does not mean the worldwide unity of the capitalist social formation, or its establishment as a single entity on a world level. Such an entity would presuppose the complete internationalization of the economic base. This would mean the integration of all national markets into an international one and the coalescing of all national divisions of labour into a worldwide division of labour. The national affiliations of capital would disappear. And there would have to be a globalization of the entire superstructure of legal, political, and other national institutions. Social consciousness would also have to become international. And a world state would have to be built to protect world capital and ensure the safety of the global production relations of a global system. Such a globalization is a tendency under capitalism today, but not one that capitalism can realize. National consciousness in regions where nations have not yet developed, efforts by oppressed nations to gain sovereignty and the existence of socialist states are too powerful obstacles to such an outcome.

Socialism, of course, is itself supposed to be a transition towards a worldwide communist system. Its very nature has in principle an internationalizing character. At the same time it is a developmental process which grew out of capitalism. But capitalism had unfolded as a national system, leading to developed national capitalisms in certain parts of the world, and as a world system suppressing national development in other parts. The construction of socialism was therefore necessarily set in motion first within a *national* framework. It drew on local national resources. It was pushed forward, or hindered, by local socio-political forces, in the context and under the impact of a still capitalist world economy. Socialism has to complete a double and contradictory task inherited from capitalism: to promote a real internationalization of the world economy, and to create or develop national economies in the world economy's periphery.

In the world transformation process, social and national emancipation must go hand in hand. This implies both *social* and *national* forces being at work. They may either reinforce or weaken each other; this depends on the actual phase of the transformation process, the interference or otherwise of external forces, and what concrete issues are on the agenda.

Issues for the Future

Particularly in the last two decades, the cumulative inequalities and disequilibria of the world economy have become self-evident. There is also a recognition of the increasing interdependence between its various parts. The inter-relations between economic, technological and ecological aspects of development are also much clearer. These developments have defeated the conventional dogmas of liberal economics about a harmonious world economy. They have dispelled illusions about consumer societies and almighty technological revolutions. And many international economists have become convinced of the need for a new approach. This is evidenced by the birth of the idea of a New International Economic Order, which has developed both as a rather eclectic ideology and as a negotiating stance in international bodies. Even the new social science exercise of global modelling has pointed in that direction.

The New International Economic Order

Although global modelling has often been related to the NIEO idea, the latter has been much less comprehensively and consistently elaborated than most global models. It is more obviously a policy-oriented platform. And there is another difference. Most world models, even when elaborated by teams consisting of scholars with diverse political and ideological views, do reflect fairly consistently a particular theoretical outlook and ideological position. But the UN documents and negotiations on the NIEO often embody opposed theoretical views and practical interests.

What seems to be, however, a common feature of both the global models which have been produced up to now and the NIEO documents and negotiations, is their neglect of the question of fundamental changes in the social relations of the world economy, i.e. a real transformation of its essential nature.

Since 1971 when Forrester's book *World Dynamics* appeared, several global models have been published. These include the Reports to the Club of Rome, Leontief's UN Input–Output Model, Herrera's Bariloche World Model, etc.,[101] and none of them (except in one sense, the latter)[102] has actually assumed profound changes and restructuring.

The idea of a New International Economic Order has got a long history. It goes back to the first UNCTAD meeting in 1964 and the Algiers Conference of the Non-Aligned Countries in 1973.[103] Its main principles, demands and proposed measures were formulated in the Declaration and Programme of Action on the Establishment of a New International Economic Order at the Sixth Special Session of the UN General Assembly in 1974. During its history, the philosophy of the NIEO has been enriched in many ways. It has been extended to cover non-economic relations, and thereby transformed into the NIO. It has been incorporated in the programmes of various UN bodies. And it has attracted the attention of the international social science literature which has produced more and more new ideas. But its original inconsistency has survived. Along with the conflicts of interest and deterioration in both world economic conditions and the political atmosphere since the late 1970s, it is the internal weaknesses and inconsistencies of the NIEO idea which seem to be largely responsible for the failure to get it implemented.

Without going into details here,[104] it is necessary to point out that some of the declared principles and practical recommendations still reflect the influence of old conventional dogmas and naïve illusions about the harmonious effects of factor mobility, aid transfers and the market mechanism. On the other hand, a great many other NIEO proposals bear the marks of an opposite approach, of theories discrediting the latter and suggesting, instead, some regulation and reform of exchange relations and transfer mechanisms. Indeed a few even raise more fundamental issues, corresponding to the conclusions of more radical theories.

Although, and perhaps precisely because, the idea of a new international economic order has been generally accepted, its meaning is the subject of many different interpretations. One interpretation,[105] expressed also in some global models, conceives of it as a programme whereby a few very powerful states will use their control over international organizations[106] to ensure some measure of appropriate re-cycling of oil revenue surpluses,[107] in order to restore equilibrium to the world market which was originally disturbed by the oil price explosion. This would involve increasing the free movement of factors of production, while reducing financial aid for poor countries to a level merely required in order to avoid conflicts or political revolts.

Another interpretation has been called by Robert Cox the 'social democratic variant of the establishment view'.[108] This puts emphasis on international welfare measures to improve the living conditions of the poorest people of the world. This would be achieved by means of expanded aid programmes and automatic income redistribution via international taxation. The proposals accept the principles of the free market and factor mobility. But they call for certain palliative reforms in exchange relations, financial and monetary systems, and a sort of indicative planning on a world level.[109] This variant seems to be closest to the reformist theories of the world economy which were perhaps the most influential in formulating the UN documents on the NIEO. They brought to the fore recommendations for improving the terms of trade, stabilizing markets and exchange rates, debt relief, and concessional aid for the poorest countries. But they did not touch on the basic roots of unequal exchange relations, indebtedness and the shortage of capital.

Besides these, there is a radical interpretation described by Cox as 'historical materialist'.[110] This focused on production structures and social relations. It argued that the fundamental inequalities and unequal development of the capitalist world economy could not be changed by minor reforms on the level of circulation (trade relations, capital flows, technology transfers etc.) and income redistribution. Instead it proposed profound changes to be carried out by revolutionary social and national forces in the social relations of world production and the structure of the international division of labour.

Wide differences, of course, appear even within the above main variants, particularly in respect of ways and means of implementation.

As regards the actual multilateral negotiations on the NIEO, it is precisely the various short-term measures, minor reforms and redistributive, palliative actions which have gained primary (often exclusive) attention, despite their more or less zero sum game character. In contrast, those issues which are related to a real transformation of world economic relations — for example, the criteria of national sovereignty in an economic sense, or the equalization of structural roles in the world economy — have been hardly negotiated at all, even if lip-service has been paid to some nice principles.

In addition to the inconsistencies within the 'basket' of NIEO principles and the above bias in the multilateral negotiations which have followed, the various elements of the programme to implement them have been treated separately from each other. Unlike most world models which apply a more or less comprehensive, global approach, the NIEO programme of implementation has been fragmented and almost departmentalized in line with the different specializations of the various UN bodies.[111]

In conclusion, it is difficult to conceive what would be really meant by a New International Economic Order as a feasible strategy for the transformation of the world economy. But at the least such a strategy would require:

★ A consistent conception which is based upon a thorough analysis of the roots of the problems;
★ A complex approach integrating the various spheres of action;
★ A co-ordinated sequence of short-term and long-term measures in which the key strategic issues would be given priority and minor reforms or badly needed palliatives would be at the service of the latter;
★ And widespread publicity for such a strategy in order to mobilize all those democratic socio-political forces in the world which understand the need for world transformation and are ready to participate actively in it, to exert pressure and fight for it.

To return briefly to a point we made at the beginning of this book, economic problems are often not only the subjects but also the causes of socio-political or international conflicts. But we can by no means reduce the key issues of the transformation of the world economy to the realm of economics alone. Nor can we reduce them to those related to the Third World or its poverty-stricken population only, however much the negative consequences of the present world order are concentrated in the developing countries and suffered primarily by their poorest people.

The Basic Issues
Nevertheless, certain key issues emerge out of the fact that fundamental and lasting inequalities in the world economy, the tendency for the development gap to widen and the underdevelopment of the Third World are rooted in the unequal, asymmetrical pattern of capital ownership and control over development resources, and in the structurally imbalanced, unequal division of labour which perpetuate asymmetrical international dependence relations. These key issues can be summarized as follows:[112]

1. *National Sovereignty:* One of them concerns national sovereignty in its full sense, i.e. in a political as well as economic and cultural sense. Emancipation of nations is a prerequisite of any real internationalization on an egalitarian basis. But it cannot be achieved without such sovereignty. It is, however, not enough to declare it. What is needed is to respect and protect it and ensure its objective conditions.

The NIEO Declaration, and particularly the Charter of Economic Rights and Duties of States, have clearly defined what sovereignty in an economic sense implies. What is now required is a sort of economic security system which would defend those nations enforcing their sovereign rights over their own economy against foreign economic intervention and hegemonic pressure.

2. *Foreign Ownership and Control:* Since national sovereignty over the economy is reduced or prevented by asymmetrical relations of economic dependence like monopolistic foreign ownership and control over important sectors of the economy, there is no other strategic solution but to eliminate monopolistic foreign capital ownership or transform foreign companies and transnational corporations into genuinely international joint enterprises mutually owned by the nations concerned, and operated and controlled by them in a more symmetrical pattern.[113]

3. *A Fundamental Restructuring of the International Division of Labour:* The unequal allocation, and recent relocation, of structural roles in the world division of labour has not only caused and reinforced the conditions of underdevelopment and dependency of the developing countries, but it also brought about a basic imbalance in the world economy. Consequently, a fundamental restructuring of the international division of labour going far beyond the present redeployment process transferring mostly outworn, technologically dependent enclave industries to the periphery, is also a basic requirement. In view of the need for full national sovereignty over national economies, such a restructuring must lead to a relatively equal distribution of the links in the vertical chain of production. It must allow each country to possess decisive links (in particular, R and D centres) in some of the dynamic industries. And it must lead to a new world division of labour which incorporates also non-economic activities and provides equal opportunities for the different nations, ethnic groups and cultural communities to develop their talents.

Such a fundamental restructuring of the international division of labour in the production of goods and services makes it necessary to apply a long-term and integrated approach. A long-term perspective on how to develop such a strategy for co-operation needs to be thought out. The same applies even more to the non-economic spheres of the division of labour.

4. *The Arms Race:* In view of the role played by the arms race and the increasing militarization of economies all over the world, not to mention the dangers this involves for the actual survival of humankind, perhaps *the* most urgent issue of the transformation process is how to stop the arms race. It is by no means only an East–West problem since military expenditures are increasingly overwhelming the development budgets of the developing

countries as well. Development resources — natural, material and intellectual resources alike — are increasingly being misused for military purposes.

A complex, integrated approach to world problems, including economic inequalities, crisis, insecurity, the development gap as well as the arms race could, perhaps, make progress in disarmament easier as well.

5. *Consumer Society:* A further important issue is related to the wasteful consumer society and its demonstration effects on the economically less developed countries. Many of the increasing difficulties and distortions in economic life, including ecological imbalances and glaring contrasts in living standards in the world, are the result of business-manipulated consumerism, the irrational rush for material goods often of value mainly for purposes of ostentation. There is a need for an effective use of tax policies, economic incentives and education to curb luxurious consumption in the countries concerned. And collective international action is also needed to correct distorted consumption patterns and limit negative demonstration effects. Consumer demand needs to be readjusted towards *real* human needs, including the cultural and intellectual ones which tend to be underrated by the consumer society.

6. *Global Planning:* Though the basic institutional units of socio-economic and political life will remain nations in the foreseeable future, there is a need to introduce some elements of indicative global planning and regulation into international life. This is necessary, even inevitable, because of the accelerating internationalization of production, increasing interdependence between the individual parts of the world economy, the global activities of transnational companies, and the growing vulnerability in sense of all parts of the world to events in other parts. Some degree of planning at a world level cannot be avoided.

Since no world state exists or is likely to arise soon, the only opportunity for the above is inter-state co-operation within the UN system. The question then arises whether the UN's present structure and system of representation will enable it to move forward in the direction of world government.

Finally, as regards the socio-political forces which can be mobilized for the transformation of the world into a more humanitarian, egalitarian and democratic order (in both social terms, and internationally), it follows, at least implicitly, from the analysis in this study that these forces are to be found in the working masses of the world who have no vested interests in domestic or international exploitation. The policies and ideologies of particular parties and states have to be assessed according to their relationship with working people. In addition to the international labour movement (including the rural proletariat, working intelligentsia and other democratic grassroots movements), which is the primary force in the struggle for social emancipation and transformation, the progressive national movements in the developing countries are playing the main role in the struggle for national emancipation. The more these two sets of forces act in concert, the better will be the prospects for the world's transformation. And let us never forget that the potential scope of these forces acting for global transformation will be much wider and richer than any narrow or over-simplified doctrine or ideology might lead us to expect. This is inevitable given both the complex, multi-dimensional character of any global transformation process and the fabric of human diversity in attitudes, interests and behaviour.

Notes

1. On the centre–periphery relations, see *inter alia* A. G. Frank, *Capitalism and Underdevelopment in Latin America*, Monthly Review Press, New York, 1967; Samir Amin, *Unequal Development*, Harvester Press, Sussex, 1976; Immanuel Wallerstein, *Historical Capitalism*, Verso, London, 1983; and T. Szentes, *The Political Economy of Underdevelopment*, Akadémiai, Budapest, 1983.

2. On the concept of semi-periphery, see Immanuel Wallerstein, *The Modern World System*, Academic Press, New York, 1974 and 1980; and 'Semi-Peripheral Countries and the Contemporary World Crisis', Paper for the CENDES Seminar, 1975.

3. See Terence K. Hopkins and Immanuel Wallerstein, 'Patterns of Development of the Modern World-System: Research Proposal', *Review*, Vol. I, No. 2, Fall 1977.

4. See T. Szentes, op. cit.

5. For a historical, comparative and critical investigation of Western non-Marxist economic theories, see Antal Mátyás, *History of Modern Non-Marxian Economics*, Akadémiai Publ., Budapest, 1980. For other surveys, see E. James, *Histoire de la pensée économique au XXᵉ siècle*, Presses Universitaires, Paris, 1955; G. Ackley, *Macro-economic Theory*, The Macmillan Co., New York, 1967; P. W. Bell and M. P. Todaro, *Economic Theory*, Oxford University Press, 1969.

6. For a critical analysis of the main theories of the world economy, see T. Szentes, *Theories of World Capitalist Economy: A Critical Survey of Conventional Reformist and Radical Views*, Akadémiai Publ., Budapest, 1985.

7. See A. Marshall, *The Pure Theory of Foreign Trade: Money, Credit and Commerce*, London, 1923.

8. See B. Ohlin, *Inter-regional and International Trade*, Cambridge, Mass., 1923, and E. F. Heckscher, 'The Effects of Foreign Trade on the Distribution of Income', *Ekonomisk Tidskrift*, 1919.

9. See, for example, W. W. Rostow, *The Stages of Economic Growth: A Non-Communist Manifesto*, Cambridge University Press, 1960.

10. For a detailed critical survey of these concepts of underdevelopment, see T. Szentes, *The Political Economy of Underdevelopment*, op. cit.

11. A few years ago Josef Pajestka and Jan Kulig produced a sweeping criticism of the dependencia school of development thinking by attributing to it the thesis of the North–South dichotomy and the suggestion that remedies for the developing countries should be applied from without. These authors seemed, however, not only to confuse the substance of the centre–periphery concept with a certain extreme interpretation of it, but also to forget that Lenin's theory of imperialism also included the concept of a centre–periphery relationship, a dichotomy between a dominant centre and an economically dependent, exploited periphery, without which imperialism could be interpreted merely (and in sharp contradiction to Lenin's warning) as a political phenomenon. Besides, it ought to be noted that the correct recognition of the primarily external causes of underdevelopment does not mean a neglect of the local, internal aspect of it, and by no means suggests necessarily an external solution only. See Josef Pajestka and Jan Kulig, 'The Socialist Countries of Eastern Europe and the New International Economic Order', *Trade and Development: An UNCTAD Review*, No. 1, 1979, UN, pp. 67–82.

12. Paul Streeten, when reviewing the development of development theories and comparing the various views on the world economy and underdevelopment, draws a line between the theories of linear development and those interpreting underdevelopment as a product of world economy. He groups under the latter both non-Marxists and Marxists, including the author of this book. See: P. Streeten: L'evolùion des théories relatives au développement économique. *Problèmes Economique*. Nov. 9. 1977.

13. Here, again, for a more detailed survey, see T. Szentes, *Theories of World Capitalist Economy*, op. cit.

14. See Gunnar Myrdal, *Economic Theory and Underdeveloped Regions*, Duckworth, London, 1957.

15. H. W. Singer, 'Distribution of Gains Between Investing and Borrowing Countries', *The American Economic Review*. May 1950; and *International Development: Growth and Change*, McGraw-Hill, 1964.

16. Raul Prebisch, 'Commercial Policy in Underdeveloped Countries', *The American Economic Review*, Papers and Proceedings, 1959; *Towards a New Trade Policy for Development*, UNCTAD, New York, 1964; and W. A. Lewis, 'Economic Development with Unlimited Supplies of Labour', in A. N. Agarwala and S. P. Singh (eds.), *The Economics of Underdevelopment*, Oxford University Press, 1958.

17. Thomas Balogh, *Unequal Partners*, Vol. I, Oxford, 1963.

18. Raul Prebisch, op. cit.

19. Celso Furtado, *External Dependence and Economic Theory*, IDEP, Repr. 272, Dakar 1971; *Obstacles to Development in Latin America*, Doubleday and Co., New York, 1970; and H. W. Singer, 'Distribution of Gains from Trade and Investment – Revisited', *First Interpag Conference*, IDS, 1971, and IDEP Repr. 270, Dakar.

20. François Perroux, *L'économie du XXème siècle*, Presses Universitaires de France, Paris, 1964.

21. Singer, 1971, op. cit.

22. See Singer's revised views, ibid.

23. Arghiri Emmanuel, *Unequal Exchange: A Study of the Imperialism of Trade*, Monthly Review Press, New York, 1972.

24. *Inter alia*, A. O. Hirschman, 'How to Divest in Latin America and Why?', *Essays in International Finance*, No. 76, Princeton University, 1969.

25. Raul Prebisch, *Change and Development – Latin America's Great Task*, IDEP/ET/CS/2367, Repr, Dakar, 1972.

26. See Samir Amin, *L'echange inégal et la loi de la valeur*, Anthropos – IDEP, Paris, 1973; *The Law of Value and Historical Materialism*, Monthly Review Press, New York, 1978; Oscar Braun, *Comercio International e Imperialismo*, Siglo XXI 1973; and Jagdish Saigal, 'Réflexions sur la Théorie de "l'échange inégal"', in S. Amin, ibid.

27. Frantz Fanon, *The Wretched of the Earth*, Penguin, London, 1967.

28. For example, just to cite one case, the significant change and progress in the thinking of Raul Prebisch, manifested in his complex critique of the system of periphery capitalism.

29. There is, of course, no central authority, like the Catholic Church and the Christian religion, which is vested with the right to make such an adjudication, and to initiate or excommunicate anybody. The only way to identify whether alleged Marxists are actually representatives of pro-capitalist or other ideologies is to reveal their objective relationship with the substantial content (not minor details or terminology) of these ideologies and their approach and methods.

By Marxism, I mean a living, developing and politically effective Marxism and not its scholastic, dogmatic remnant let alone the falsification of its very content under the guise of terminology. The substance of Marxism implies an historical approach, a dialectical and holistic method and an admitted class viewpoint to be applied in the analysis of social phenomena. This means a committed stand taken in favour of the working, exploited and oppressed classes, looking for their interests *vis-à-vis* their exploiters and oppressors — i.e. a real and active humanism. There are also a few fundamental theoretical principles such as the labour theory of value in political economy, the concept of social relations of production as the 'base' of social systems and class formation, the recognition of class struggle as a motive force in history, the relationship between existence and consciousness in dialectical and historical materialism, and so on that do characterize real Marxism.

30. Karl Marx, *Capital*, Foreign Languages Publishing House, Moscow, 1966–68.

31. Hilferding, *Finanzkapital*, Berlin, 1947; V. I. Lenin, *Imperialism: The Highest Stage of Capitalism*, in *Selected Works*, Moscow, Progress, 1968; J. A. Hobson, *Imperialism*, Nisbet, 1902; R. Luxemburg, *The Accumulation of Capital*, London, Routledge and Kegan Paul, 1951; N. Bukharin, *Imperialism and the World Economy*, London, Merlin, 1970; K. Kautsky, *The Dictatorship of the Proletariat*, Ann Arbor, Univ. of Michigan Press, 1964; L. Trotsky, *The Permanent Revolution*, 1928, and *Result and Prospects*, 1906, London, New Park Publications, 1962.

32. V. I.Lenin, *Imperialism: The Highest Stage of Capitalism*, op. cit.

33. See J. Pajestka and J. Kulig in Note 11 above.

34. See Stalin's argument that the world market was now split into two separate markets: a capitalist and a socialist one. J. Stalin, *Economic Problems of Socialism in the U.S.S.R.*, Foreign Languages Publishing House, Moscow, 1953.

35. Paul Baran, *The Political Economy of Growth*, Prometheus, New York, 1957; A. G. Frank, *Capitalism and Underdevelopment in Latin America: Historical Studies of Chile and Brazil*, Monthly Review Press, New York 1967; Samir Amin, *Accumulation on a World Scale*, Monthly Review Press, New York, 1974.

36. Immanuel Wallerstein, *The Modern World System: Capitalist Agriculture and the Origins of the European World Economy in the Sixteenth Century*, Academic Press, New York, San Francisco, London, 1974; 'The Rise and Future Demise of the World Capitalist System: Concepts for Comparative Analysis', Paper for the Annual Meeting of the American Sociological Association, New Orleans, 1972; 'A world system perspective on the social sciences', *The British Journal of Sociology*, 1976, Vol. 27, No. 3; and Terence K. Hopkins and Immanuel Wallerstein, 'Patterns of Development of the Modern World System: Research Proposal', *Review*, 1977, Vol. I, No. 2.

37. The identification of capitalism with the market economy has become a fashionable concept which, though stemming from the illusions of classical bourgeois economics about spontaneous market forces and coming into increasing contradiction with the reality of monopolistic power and state intervention (called as 'market imperfections'), influences even some Marxist scholars. Samir Amin, for one, assumes that, since the objective economic laws which operate through the actions of individuals are attached only to the market economy (i.e. to capitalism), neither pre-capitalistic societies nor socialism have objective economic laws.

No doubt, capitalism, by commercializing human labour and natural resources, has carried commodification to extremes, and even put moral and cultural values up on sale. But the substantive pre-condition for doing so has been the separation, by means of the institution of private ownership, of producers from the other means of production. Exchange relations and markets existed before capitalism, and the transformation of the capitalist system into a socialist one can hardly be implemented by eliminating the market (as is shown by the abortive attempts of the Pol Pot government in Cambodia).

38. The late President Chernenko urged Soviet social scientists to asess more realistically what levels of socialist development had actually been achieved in the Soviet Union. He suggested that Soviet society was still in a relatively *early* phase of the long historical process leading to a fully developed socialist society. This point has been even more strongly emphasized by the present Secretary-General, Mikhail Gorbachev.

39. Those holding this view often call the existing socialist system 'state socialism'.

40. The resolutions of party congresses in the socialist countries have been stressing for a long time now the manifold varieties of socialist paths of development that exist and their local and national specificities, as well as the need of all countries to learn from one another. It was Lenin, after all, who stressed that a complete socialism stemming from the revolutionary co-operation of the proletariat of the whole world would be the outcome of a number of experiments, each of which would be in itself biased and unharmonious.

41. Bettelheim became disillusioned by the gap between ideal socialism and existing socialist societies. As a result, he argued that Soviet society as well as the Chinese, Cuban and Vietnamese societies have all remained capitalist. He even redefines the 1917 Revolution

retrospectively and all subsequent ones as capitalist revolutions. See C. Bettelheim, *Class Struggles in the USSR, 1930–41*, Monthly Review Press, New York, 1984.

42. On the stages of development research, see D. Senghaas and Menzel, 'Autocentric development despite international competence differentials', *Economics* Vol. 21, 1980.

43. See, in particular, B. Warren, *Imperialism, Pioneer of Capitalism*, London, Verso, 1980.

44. Samir Amin, 'Expansion or Crisis of Capitalism', (xerox), 1983; and A. Liepitz, 'Marx or Rostow', *New Left Review*, No. 132, 1982.

45. See e.g. J. Pajestka–J. Kulig: The socialist countries of Eastern Europe and the New International Economic Order. *Trade and Development: An UNCTAD Review*. No. 1. 1979.

46. As is well-known, many historians deny that history has shown any objective tendencies or 'laws'. The concept of development in a particular direction may be repudiated even by those who recognize certain laws in history but not necessarily as laws of progress. For a comparison of the views concerned, see D. K. Fieldhouse, 'Some conclusions: the historian and the historicists' in D. K. Fieldhouse (ed), *The Theory of Capitalist Imperialism*, Longman, London, 1967; and Gavin Williams, 'Imperialism and Development: A Critique', in *World Development*, 1978, Vol. 6, pp. 925–36. For a critique of 'developmentalism', see Terence K. Hopkins and Immanuel Wallerstein, op. cit.

47. For one of the exceptions, see note 11 above.

48. See, for example, H. Magdoff, 'Imperialism – A Historical Survey', *Monthly Review*, Vol. 24, May 1972; A. G. Frank, *Capitalism and Underdevelopment in Latin America*, Monthly Review Press, New York, 1967; S. H. Hymer and S. A. Resnick, *International Trade and Uneven Development*. IDEP, 271. Dakar, October 1971; O. Sunkel, *Development, Underdevelopment, Dependence, Marginality and Special Imbalances – Towards a Global Approach*, IDEP, Repr. 269, Dakar, 1971; A. Arrighi, 'International Corporations, Labour Aristocracies and Economic Development in Tropical Africa', in G. Arrighi and J. S. Saul, *Essays on the Political Economy of Africa*, Monthly Review Press, New York, 1973.

49. Samir Amin, *Unequal Development*, Monthly Review Press, New York, 1976.

50. See Dieter Senghaas, *The European Experience: A Historical Critique of Development Theory*, Berg Publishers, Leamington Spa and Dover, New Hampshire, 1985.

51. N. D. Kondratieff, 'The Long Waves in Economic Life', in *The Review of Economic Statistics*, Cambridge, USA, 1935; J. A. Schumpeter, *Business Cycles*, New York, McGraw Hill, 1939; J. B. Shuman and D. Rosenau, *The Kondratieff Wave*, New York, World Publishing, 1972; Simon Kuznets, *Secular Trends in Production and Prices*, Boston, 1930; E. Kemenes, 'Cyclical and Secular Changes in the World Economy', in *Trends in World Economy*, Hungarian Scientific Council for World Economy, No. 35, Budapest, 1981. We cannot go into detail here to discuss the different views on the Kondratieff waves, business cycles and various other types of crisis. Nor can we discuss what has been called the general crisis of capitalism, beginning in 1917 and caused by the rise of socialist regimes. What, however, is necessary to note is that, besides the normal business cycles originating in the developed national economies, the capitalist world economy has also undergone, more or less regularly, periods of expansion and of contraction. Since the birth of socialist states, these cycles and tendencies have been affected by the existence of these regimes.

52. See Karl Polányi, Conrad M. Arensberg and Harry W. Pearson (eds.), *Trade and Market in the Early Empires*, Free Press and Falcon Wing Press, Glencoe, 1957.

53. On this important, though perhaps over-simplified, distinction between the two trade patterns, see I. Wallerstein, 'The Three Stages of African Involvement in the World Economy', in Peter C. W. Gutkind and Immanuel Wallerstein (eds.), *The Political Economy of Contemporary Africa*, Vol. I, Sage Series on African Modernization and Development, Beverly Hills/London, 1976, pp. 30–57.

54. Jan Otto Andersson distinguishes between the historical stage of a 'capitalist world market' and that of the 'world capitalist economy'. See J. O. Andersson, *Studies in the Theory of Unequal Exchange Between Nations*, ABO, No. 9, Helsinki, 1976, pp. 56–64.

55. It is really puzzling why several Marxist and New Left scholars who otherwise strongly oppose the bourgeois liberal concept of the world economy as a mere juxtaposition of autonomous national economies, do not see the significance of international ownership relations stemming from the export of investment capital. Instead, they reduce the relations of

dependence and exploitation between centre and periphery to unequal international trade and specialization. Such a reduction presupposes either the permanent use of purely non-economic force against the periphery or a voluntary and servile adjustment of the latter to the economic interests of the centre.

One can argue, of course, that this neglect of ownership relations is due to the correct recognition by these scholars of the fact that Western monopoly capital, particularly the transnational corporations today, can exert control over the economy of a given country in the periphery without full or even partial ownership of equity capital. However, even in this case, such neglect reflects a narrowing down of the meaning of capital ownership and a disregard of history, reflection on which would show how behind what is possible today, lies what was necessary yesterday. It also manifests a confusion that what is feasible in particular cases must therefore be possible in all countries — which is a contradiction of the world system approach itself.

56. One of the most serious errors, even deliberate manipulations, is the attribution of this spirit to the general and inherited quality of European people as a race. This false notion of a sort of European way of thinking and behaviour neglects the historical context of the birth of capitalism. Certainly the latter cannot be explained by such a spirit.

57. See Anouar Abdel-Malek, 'Sociology and economic history: an essay on mediation', in Peter Gutkind and Peter Waterman (eds.), *African Social Studies: A Radical Reader*, Monthly Review Press, New York and London, 1977, pp. 62–75.

58. A. G. Frank, *Capitalism and Underdevelopment in Latin America*, Monthly Review Press, New York, 1967, 1969.

59. Professors Berend and Ránki, two Hungarian economic historians, have done intensive research on the regions of the European periphery, the so-called second edition of feudalism in Eastern Europe and the reactions of the ruling classes, in general, in Eastern and Southern Europe to the challenge of Western industrialism, as well as the particular paths of capitalist development of the latecomer countries in the 19th century. Berend T. Iván and Ránki György, *Gazdasági elmaradottság: Kiutak és kudarcok a XIX.századi Európában (Economic Underdevelopment: Get-outs and Failures in 19th century Europe)*, Közgazdasági, Budapest, 1979.

60. We use the term dualism in its socio-economic sense, meaning a dualistic, dichotomous structure consisting of two main, characteristic but different socio-economic sectors: a capitalist, modern one and a pre-capitalist, traditional one. These two sectors do not simply co-exist but are also in a sort of internal centre–periphery relationship in which the traditional sector is subordinated to the modern one and fulfils certain functions for the latter, losing thereby its genuine original character. In the relevant international literature, there also exist other interpretations of dualism in which it is confined to mere differences in sociological characteristics or technological parameters. For the various interpretations of dualism, see J. H. Boeke, *Economics and Economic Policy of Dual Societies*, New York, 1953; Benjamin Higgins, 'The Dualistic Theory of Underdeveloped Areas', *Economic Development and Cultural Change*, January 1956; Howard S. Ellis, 'Dual Economies and Progress', in *Revista de Economia Latinoamericana*, 1962; Samir Dasgupta, 'Underdevelopment and Dualism: A Note', *EDDC*, No. 12, 1964; A. O. Hirschman, 'Investment Policies and Dualism in Underdeveloped Countries', *The American Economic Review*, September 1957; Ignacy Sachs, *Patterns of Public Sector in Underdeveloped Economies*, Asia Publishing House, London, 1964; Tamás Szentes, *The Political Economy of Underdevelopment*, Akadémiai Budapest, 1971, 1973, 1976, 1983. For a critique of the narrow and static conceptions of dualism, see T. Szentes, 'Une interpretation restreinte du dualisme dans les théories du sous-développement', *Études sur les pays en voie de développement*, No. 45, Budapest, 1971.

61. A. G. Frank, *Lumpenbourgeoisie and Lumpendevelopment: Dependency, Class and Politics in Latin America*, New York, Monthly Review Press, 1972.

62. See Catherine Coquéry-Vidrovitch, 'De l'impérialisme ancien a l'impérialisme moderne: l'avatar colonial', in *Sociologie de l'imperialisme*, Anthropos, Paris, 1971; J. A. Schumpeter, *The Sociology of Imperialism: Imperialism and Social Classes*, Meridian, New York, 1951; A. Emmanuel, 'White-Settler Colonialism and the Myth of Investment Imperialism', *New Left Review*, 1972, No. 73.

63. Marxist theory distinguishes between two forms of capital export: loan capital (which is redeemed within a specified repayment period and bears interest), and working capital (which is invested in the recipient country's economy, and which perpetuates and expands itself by reinvestment of some of the profits that result). Exported working capital is therefore more or less equal in volume to so-called foreign direct investments plus those portfolio investments which are made indirectly by private capitalists in a foreign country.

64. This separation of capital ownership from capital activity, and thus the distinction between owner and managing entrepreneur, has been made possible by the institution of the holding company.

65. Surplus capital means relatively superfluous, idle capital which, under given business conditions, cannot find sufficient profitable investment opportunities. The relativity of this phenomenon lies in the fact that the expected rate of profit is the primary criterion for investing accumulated capital under the conditions of an economy based upon private ownership. If, however, investment decisions are no longer in private hands or no longer depend only on a private or micro-level calculus of profitability, then surplus capital may disappear since the scope for socially useful (and socially profitable) investments normally exceeds the available capital funds.

66. Samir Amin, *Unequal Exchange*, op. cit.

67. For more details, see T. Szentes, *The Political Economy of Underdevelopment*, op. cit.

68. See ibid. for a detailed analysis of the consequences of a disintegrated, dualistic socio-economic structure for domestic market relations, capital formation, employment and training, the 'population explosion', and class relations.

69. We may note here that capital export may not necessarily lead to the above consequences. Where a fairly powerful and active local, national capital supported by a nation state exists, national capital may be capable of preventing the inflowing foreign capital from seizing the commanding heights of the economy or achieving a monopolistic position. It is true, however, that such cases do not follow from the inherent tendencies of capital export, but on the contrary, from the intensity of counter-tendencies.

70. A comprador bourgeoisie is distinguished from the national bourgeoisie by its servile attitude (based, as a rule, on business interests) towards foreign capital and imperialist power. Those elements of the local bourgeoisie which take an interest in establishing national industry can be regarded, almost by definition, as the national bourgeoisie in those cases where industrial development in the periphery has been systematically blocked by metropolitan power.

71. The meaning of the term equivalence or equality of international exchange is a widely debated issue. Apart from the various immanent inequalities of exchange such as those resulting from differing levels of productivity, wages, or factor proportions (capital intensity), a clear case of the violation of exchange equality exists when the periphery countries are forced by monopolies to pay higher than world market prices for their imports, or receive lower than world prices for their exports.

72. Structural inequalities are not easy to define. It is, however, obvious that in a country with a limited production structure (i.e. lacking leading and dynamic industries), the key links in the vertical chain of production are in a weaker, unequal, position compared to other countries. It is also obvious that where a nation's productivity is prevented by such structural deficiencies and the shortage of skilled labour from catching up with that of its trading partners, the country has to pay, as a rule, more labour in exchange for less from its partners.

73. Since this study focuses primarily on the socio-economic aspects of the world transformation process, we cannot discuss in detail the changes in the pattern and behaviour of political forces here.

74. During the Cold War, the isolation of the economies of Eastern Europe from the Western economies — which was an abnormal situation from the point of view of their traditional historical relations with each other and the objective tendencies towards internationalization — was the result of the policy of economic autarky which prevailed in the Eastern European socialist states at the time. This situation gave birth to, and was ideologically supported by, Stalin's idea of a split in the world market into two — a capitalist and a socialist one. See J. Stalin, op. cit.

75. It would go beyond the scope of this study of investigate this process, its results and shortcomings, progress and deviations, objective difficulties and the subjective errors of economic policy pursued in its various periods, as well as the differences in individual cases. Nevertheless we should note that changes in the economic policies and management systems of the East European socialist countries have become necessary because of the various tensions and bottlenecks which followed from mistakes in previous economic policy, including over-centralization, the growth of bureaucracy, and over-investment, etc., and also because manpower resources have been increasingly exhausted by the extensive stage of economic growth. A change-over to an intensive stage with an emphasis on the qualitative aspects of production (unit costs, quality and productivity) will inevitably follow from re-linking and more or less normalized and expanding trade relations with the capitalist economies, and the increased participation of the socialist countries in the international division of labour. Greater flexibility in their economic systems, increased responsiveness to consumer demand and market changes, and more decentralized management and decision-making systems will also follow.

76. There already exists a huge international literature on TNCs, in which we can find diametrically opposed and extreme views, ranging all the way from accusations that they are the devils incarnate of today which ought to be exorcised by a naïvely presumed return to smaller, national, competitive firms, to adulatory praise for them as the most appropriate, progressive forms of international economic co-operation. For a critique of both viewpoints, see T. Szentes, 'The TNC Issue: Naïve Illusions or Exorcism and Lip-Service?', *Review*, Vol. VI, No. 2, Fall 1982.

77. Richard R. Weiner, 'Pluralism and neo-corporatism: the legacy of the New Deal and the "social contract"', *XIIIth World Congress of Political Science*, IPSA, Paris, 1985, p. 2.

78. Samir Amin, 'Expansion or Crisis of Capitalism?', Mimeo, p. 25.

79. Richard R. Weiner, op. cit, p. 20.

80. M. Dauderstädt and A. Pfaller, 'The New Zero-Sum World', *Analysis and Information*, FES, Bonn, 1985.

81. For more detailed analyses of the changes in the pattern of foreign direct investment and the international division of labour, see A. Seidman, 'Old Motives, New Methods: Foreign Enterprise in Africa Today', *African Perspectives*, Cambridge University Press, 1970; G. Arrighi, 'International Corporations, Labour Aristocracies and Economic Development in Tropical Africa', in G. Arrighi and J. Saul, *Essays on the Political Economy of Africa*, Monthly Review Press, 1973, pp.105–151; V. Tyagunenko, 'Neocolonialism and the international capitalist division of labour', *International Affairs*, 1971, No. 1, p. 12; J. Leontiades, 'International Sourcing in the LDCs', *Columbia Journal of World Business*, Vol. VI, No. 6, 1971, pp. 20–21; B. Brown, 'New Trends in Trade and Investment', *International Seminar on Imperialism*, Paper No. 3, New Delhi, 1972; F. Fröbel, J. Heinrichs and O. Keye, 'Tendency towards a New International Division of Labour: Worldwide Utilisation of Labour Force for World Market Oriented Manufacturing', *Economic and Political Weekly*, Bombay, February 1976; T. Szentes, 'Socio-economic Effects of Two Patterns of Foreign Capital Investments, with Special Reference to East Africa', in Peter C. W. Gutkind and Immanuel Wallerstein (eds.) *The Political Economy of Contemporary Africa*, Sage, 1976, Ch. 11; T. Szentes, 'Structural roots of the employment problem', *International Social Science Journal*, Vol. XXVIII, No. 4, 1976; T. Szentes, 'Transnationals Impede Industrialization and Sovereignty of Developing Countries', *New Perspectives*, No. 4, 1979.

82. In a few countries of Latin America, where the local bourgeoisie had become stronger much earlier than in other developing areas, this type of industrialization started already between the two world wars. The fiasco that ensued has been widely acknowledged in both official documents and scholarly papers. See, among others, the writings of Raul Prebisch and also some ECLA Reports. One of the most clear-cut theoretical appraisals can be found in A. G. Frank, *Lumpenbourgeoisie and Lumpendevelopment: Dependency, Class and Politics in Latin America*, Monthly Review Press, New York, 1972.

83. Samir Amin, *L'échange inégal*, op. cit.

84. For a critique of such an over-simplification, see Szentes, 'The TNCs Issue . . .', op. cit.

85. Charles Oman, 'Changing international investment strategies in the North–South

context', *The CTC Reporter*, Centre on Transnational Corporations, No. 22, Autumn 1986, New York, p. 47.

86. UNCTAD, *Trade and Development Report, 1986*, UN, New York, 1986, pp. 11, 32–35.

87. Otto Kreye and Alexander Schubert, 'Social Implications of Third World Debt', Public Services International Conference on Public Service Workers, Social and Economic Crisis, and the Role of International Financial Institutions, Geneva, 4–6 November 1986.

88. UN, *Living Conditions in Developing Countries in the mid-1980s: Supplement to the 1985 Report on the World Social Situation*, UN, New York, 1986, p. 2.

89. For a more detailed explanation see T. Szentes, 'Challenges of the Global Economic Crisis and World Economic Effects: The Case of Eastern Europe', UNU Research Report, RGSD Project on Peace and Global Transformation, 1985.

90. Kálmán Kulcsár, 'Politics in the Central-East-European Region: A socio-historical sketch', in *Underdevelopment and Modernization*, Working Papers, Institute of Sociology, HAS, Budapest, 1982, p. 22.

91. For an excellent analysis of the cyclical movements of the developed capitalist economies, their downturn since 1967, the inflationary tendencies connected with US military expenditures and the way they have been financed, as the background of the world crisis in early 1970s, see Andre Gunder Frank, *Crisis in the World Economy*, Heinemann, London, 1980. Where we, perhaps, disagree, is his order of priorities among the causes of the crisis. These, however, may reflect the unique nature of this crisis and how it ought to be distinguished from all the previous ones, including the 1929 worldwide crisis.

92. T. Szentes, 'Global nature, origins and strategic implications of the world economic crisis: An Eastern European view', *Trade and Development: An UNCTAD Review*, No. 4, Winter 1982, UN, New York. For a more detailed explanation see T. Szentes, 'The Global Crisis of the World Economy', UNU Research Paper on Peace and Global Transformation, 1984, p. 89.

93. This contradiction is, of course, in addition to the antagonistic contradiction between the increasingly social character of reproduction and its continued private ownership.

94. This is the reason why the socialist states should be economically interested and ready to participate in the efforts to overcome the world economic crisis even if it originates in capitalism. If this surprises some leftist radicals, it is probably because they neglect, by concentrating on the world revolution only, not only the national responsibilities of these states to their own peoples, but also the dialectical relationship (unity and contradiction) between the national and international aspects of the world transformation from capitalism to socialism.

95. See, for example, J. W. Forrester, *World Dynamics*, Wright-Allen Press, Cambridge, Mass., 1971; and D. and D. Meadows, *The Limits to Growth*, Universe Books, New York, 1972.

96. UNCTAD, *Trade and Development Report 1986*, op. cit.

97. See Otto Kreye and Alexander Schubert, op. cit.

98. Since the working class in a broader but Marxian sense involves all those who have to sell their own labour (whether physical or intellectual), the labour movement is not to be interpreted as restricted to manual workers only.

99. T. Szentes, 'Socio-political forces and ideologies in the world transformation process', op. cit.

100. While some radical representatives of dependency theory are inclined to deny any positive effects of the external factors, and underestimate the role of domestic forces in the development of peripheral capitalism, it is precisely the latter, i.e. the very distortion of capitalist development, which is completely neglected by those believing that imperialism has been the 'pioneer of capitalism'.

101. Instead of a full list, let us refer to the most outstanding and widely debated contributions: D. Meadows, et al., *The Limits to Growth*, Universe Books, New York, 1972; D. Meadows, et al., *The Dynamics of Growth in a Finite World*, Wright-Allen Press, Mass., 1974; M. Mesarovic and E. Pestel, *Mankind at the Turning Point: The Second Report to the Club of Rome*, Reader's Digest, 1974; H. Chenery et al., *Redistribution with Growth*, World Bank, Washington DC, 1974; A. Herrera et al., *Catastrophe or New Society? A Latin American World*

Model, IDRC, Ottawa, 1976; J. Tinbergen et al., *Reshaping the International Order: A Report to the Club of Rome*, E. P. Dutton, New York, 1976; W. Leontief et al., *The Future of the World Economy*, United Nations Study, Oxford University Press, New York, 1977; *Interfutures Facing the Future: Mastering the Probable and Managing the Unpredictable*, Research Project on the Future Development of Advanced Industrial Societies in Harmony with that of Developing Countries: Final Report, OECD, Paris, 1979; Y. Kaya et al., *Future of Global Interdependence*, 5th Global Modelling Conference, IIASA, Vienna, 1977; F. Kile and A. Rabehl, *A Value-Driven, Regionalised World Model*, 5th Global Modelling Conference, IIASA, Vienna, 1977; and S. Gupta and R. Padula, *A Global Model for Inter-regional, Inter-temporal Analysis of Trade, Capital Flows and Development*, EAPD, World Bank, Washington DC, 1978.

102. Namely in the sense that the Bariloche Model is based on the assumption of an egalitarian distribution system without, however, attempting 'to trace its development' (Krishnayya, 1979, p. 20). For a short but comprehensive critique of the various world models, see J. A. Krishnayya, *Global modelling – what does it offer?*, UNESCO Meeting of Experts on Research on the Idea of Integrated Development, Quito, 1979, UNESCO SS-79/Conf. 612/6, Paris.

103. For a pre-history of NIEO, see UNITAR, *A New International Economic Order: Selected Documents*, 1945-1975.

104. For further explanation, see T. Szentes, 'The strategic issues of NIEO and Global Negotiations', *Second Congress of the Association of Third World Economists*, Havana, April 26-30, 1981, p. 32.

105. Robert W. Cox calls it the establishment perspective which could be characterized as 'monopolistic liberalism'. He gives a comprehensive survey of the different ideologies and conceptions of the NEIO, and masterfully points to the critical differences between them. He does, however, mix up the ideological and geopolitical origins of the differing views. See Robert C. Cox, 'Ideologies and the New International Economic Order: Reflections on Some Recent Literature', *International Organization*, Vol. 33, No. 2, Spring 1979, University of Wisconsin, pp. 257-302.

106. Such a view appears, for example, in the Report of the Trilateral Commission: *Towards a Renovated International System*, The Triangle Papers 14, New York, 1977. It says: 'Some group of nations will have to take the responsibility for insuring that the international system functions effectively . . . notably some of its key states.' (pp. 41-42). It also advises the developing countries to welcome foreign-owned firms.

A similar stand was taken by the British Government when reacting to the Brandt Commission's Report. See *Extracts from Ministerial Statements and the Memorandum prepared by the Foreign and Commonwealth Office for the Overseas Development Sub-Committee of the Foreign Affairs Committee*, in 'Britain on Brandt', *IDS Bulletin*, April 1981, Vol. 12, No. 2, pp. 7-15.

107. Edward Heath, 'One Year After Brandt', *IDS Bulletin*, op. cit., p. 4.

108. R. W. Cox, op. cit., pp. 261-262, and 274-280.

109. Such ideas were to be seen in Tinbergen's RIO Report and also the Brandt Commission's Report, *North-South: A Programme for Survival*, The Report of the Independent Commission on International Development Issues under the Chairmanship of Willy Brandt, Pan Books, London and Sydney, 1980.

110. R. W. Cox, op. cit., pp. 265-6 and 289-300.

111. For a more detailed critique of these inconsistencies and weaknesses, see T. Szentes, 'The Strategic Issues of NIEO and Global Negotiations', op. cit.

112. For more details concerning the strategic issues of NIEO, see T. Szentes, op. cit., and also 'Crisis and Internal Inequalities of the World Capitalist Economy and the Third Development Decade', *Development and Peace*, Vol. 1, No. 1, 1980; and 'The New International Economic Order: Redistribution or Restructuring?' in C. T. Saunders (ed.), *East-West-South: Economic Interactions between Three Worlds*, The Macmillan Press, London, 1981, Chapter 16.

113. Ibid.

Index